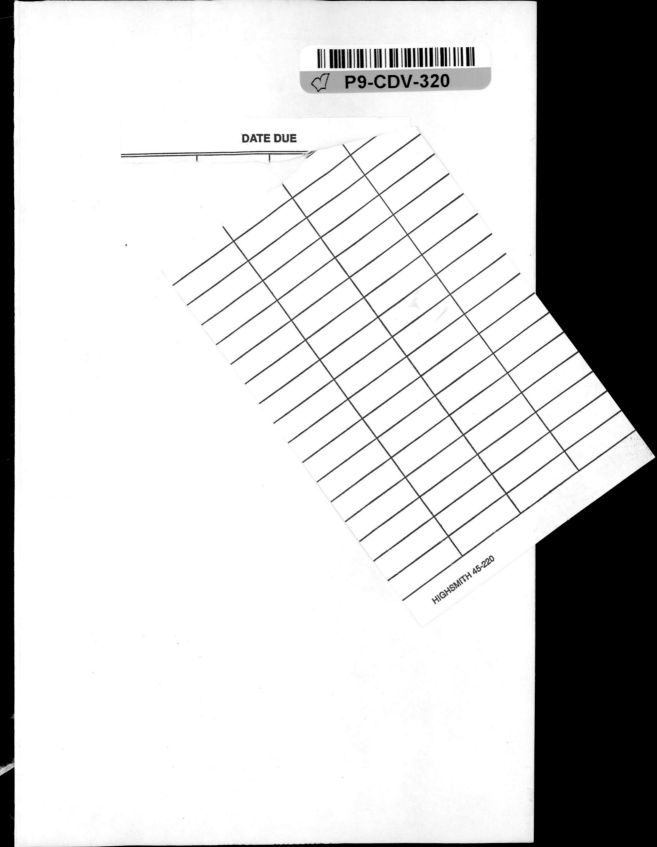

LABOR RELATIONS AND PUBLIC POLICY SERIES

REPORT NO. 13

NLRB AND JUDICIAL CONTROL OF UNION DISCIPLINE

by

THOMAS J. KEELINE

INDUSTRIAL RESEARCH UNIT
The Wharton School, Vance Hall/CS
University of Pennsylvania 19174
U.S.A.

+

Foreword

In 1968, the Industrial Research Unit inaugurated its Labor Relations and Public Policy monographs as a means of examining issues and stimulating discussions in the complex and controversial areas of collective bargaining and the regulation of labor-management disputes. The first four studies, and the eighth, ninth, and twelfth, in the series dealt with aspects of the National Labor Relations Board and its administration. The fifth report contained papers read at the fiftieth anniversary conference of the Industrial Research Unit at which many aspects of labor relations and public policy were discussed. The sixth monograph—*Welfare and Strikes*—was the first empirical analysis of the impact of government payments to strikers on the American collective bargaining system and on the settlement of disputes under that system. The seventh in the series, *Opening the Skilled Construction Trades to Blacks,* was the initial attempt to determine, by detailed field analysis, what actually occurs when the federal government insists that the skilled construction trades make a serious effort to increase the number and percentage of Negroes in their work force. The tenth, *The Davis-Bacon Act,* dealt with another aspect of construction in that it involved a critical analysis of the impact and administration of the little known law under which "prevailing wages" are established in the construction industry. The eleventh monograph in the series marked the Industrial Research Unit's first published work in the public employee field since 1966.

This, the thirteenth, examines the difficult and serious problems which arise when a union attempts to discipline a member because of an alleged infraction of union rules. The issues have come to the forefront—in many cases, have been exacerbated—since the famous U.S. Supreme Court case, *Allis-Chalmers Mfg. Co.,* 388 U.S. 175 (1967). As a result of this case, unions are able under certain conditions to sue members to collect fines which they have levied. An increasing amount of litigation has been processed refining this new union power over members.

As the author points out, the initial legal forum for resolutions of disputes involving union discipline was the various state courts. Then Congress took a hand, first through the

iii

passage of the Taft-Hartley Act in 1947, then by the enactment of the Landrum-Griffin Act of 1959. The principal litigation arena thus became the National Labor Relations Board and the federal courts. This study examines first the early state court experience, then the federal substantive (Taft-Hartley) and procedural (Landrum-Griffin) laws, and finally the current role of the state courts. The concluding chapter suggests changes in the law, its interpretation, and administration which will ensure greater protection of individual rights.

The author of this monograph, Thomas J. Keeline, Esq., received a Bachelor of Science in Economics, cum laude, from the Undergraduate Division of the University of Pennsylvania's Wharton School, and a Juris Doctor from the University's Law School. He is a member of the Missouri Bar. He served as a legal research assistant on the Industrial Research Unit's staff and is the twenty-sixth author of a Unit publication who completed a monograph while a student.

The manuscript was read by Janice R. Bellace, Esq., Robert E. Williams, Esq., and by Professor Clyde W. Summers, all of whom made constructive suggestions. The author also owes much to the pathbreaking prior research of Professor Summers. Thanks are also due to Mrs. Marie A. Dwyer, Miss Mary M. Booker, and Miss Linda J. Henzel for typing the manuscript; to Rochelle R. Bookspan and Mr. Michael J. McGrath for editing it and preparing the index; and to Mrs. Margaret E. Doyle, Office Manager, for handling administrative problems. The research was financed by the Industrial Research Unit's unrestricted funds provided by the sixty companies which comprise the Unit's Research Advisory Group. Publication was made possible by unrestricted grants from the Rollin M. Gerstacker Foundation and the Atlantic Richfield Corporation. The author is, of course, solely responsible for the research and for the views expressed, which should in no way be attributed to the grantors or to the University of Pennsylvania.

HERBERT R. NORTHRUP, *Director*
Industrial Research Unit
The Wharton School
University of Pennsylvania

Philadelphia

March 1976

TABLE OF CONTENTS

CHAPTER I

Introduction

Labor unions share similar goals with their members. The union is essentially designed, after all, to promote the welfare of its members. Nevertheless, it is fallacious to assume that the interests and rights of the members are always synonymous with those of the unions.

> Congress in 1959 enacted the Landrum-Griffin Act [Labor-Management Reporting and Disclosure Act] [1] because individual rights were being flagrantly disregarded by union officials and unions. Moreover, even if a union is fairly, accurately, and honestly acting in behalf of a majority, a minority can be genuinely aggrieved and possess rights distinctly and thoroughly different from those of the majority. . . . [2]

Policy and personality differences may also give rise to differences between union officials and members concerning the means to achieve their mutual goals. When such conflicts occur, union officials may attempt to pressure dissident members into acceptance of their policies or tactics by threatening to discipline them. Equally important, the discipline imposed on one member may chill the desire of other members to exercise their rights.

Two important conflicting needs must somehow be reconciled. On the one hand, the individual union member must be permitted to pursue his trade, to earn a living for himself and his family. He must also be allowed to participate in the affairs of the union which has a significant impact on his life, and he must be allowed to exercise his rights of free speech and dissent. Additionally, he must be free from discipline except when it is imposed after he has been found guilty of some clear, particularized, legitimate offense in a fair hearing.

The union as an institution, on the other hand, also has basic needs. If it is to be effective representing its members, it must be able to maintain a reasonably united front. It must rep-

---

[1] 73 Stat. 519 (1959), *as amended*, 29 U.S.C. §§ 401-531 (1970).

[2] H. NORTHRUP, BOULWARISM 135 (1965).

resent all of its members, and in order to serve the common good, it must exercise some degree of control over those members who disagree with majority actions and policies duly and fairly derived.

Originally, the state courts were the forums in which, as a last resort, these competing needs were balanced and reconciled. These courts struggled to find some theory to balance adequately both interests. They have at present somewhat uniformly adopted a contract theory under which they view the relationship of the member to his union as contractual. The union's constitution and bylaws are considered to be the terms of the contract. The courts will enforce the provisions of the "contract" as long as the provisions do not violate public policy and are enforced in a manner that does not violate the courts' sense of fair play.

In 1947, Congress became involved in this balancing process by passing the Labor-Management Relations Act (Taft-Hartley Act).[3] By defining union unfair labor practices, the Act disallows union interference with the job rights of members. The Act can prohibit the union from causing the discharge of those suspended or expelled. The National Labor Relations Board and the federal courts, in interpreting the Act, have been forced to find a theory to reconcile the Congressional intent of removing some conduct from union disciplinary action to the seemingly contrary Congressional intent to permit unions to regulate their own internal affairs. The Supreme Court has faced this issue on three occasions, and, in the most recent case, it indicated that the Act:

> . . . leaves a union free to enforce a properly adopted rule which reflects a legitimate union interest, impairs no policy Congress has imbedded in the labor laws, and is reasonably enforced against union members who are free to leave the union and escape the rule.[4]

In 1959, Congress passed another law in an effort to afford the members of unions more democracy and protection from improper union actions—the Landrum-Griffin Act. This Act guarantees, among other things, that a union will afford a member certain procedural safeguards in any disciplinary action against him.

This monograph examines the development of the substantive and procedural law regulating union discipline of members. Chap-

---

[3] 61 Stat. 136 (1947), *as amended*, 29 U.S.C. §§ 141 *et seq.* (1970).

[4] Scofield v. NLRB, 394 U.S. 423, 430, 70 L.R.R.M. 3105, 3108 (1969).

ter II discusses the state courts' intervention into union disciplinary proceedings and then examines the substantive rules that such courts have developed. Chapter III traces the development, rationale, and present status of the federal substantive law. Chapter IV analyzes the federal procedural law and its limits. Chapter V explores the current role of the state courts in light of federal regulation, and the final chapter presents the author's conclusions and recommendations.

CHAPTER II

State Law And Internal Union Affairs

Long before the federal government began regulating union discipline of members, state courts began hearing such cases.[1] The state courts, however, traditionally have been reluctant to intervene in the internal affairs of unions.[2] This reluctance is based on the premise that labor unions are voluntary associations similar to religious or fraternal associations. Given the power, size, and significance of modern labor unions, such analogies have been increasingly considered invalid.

In order to overcome their reluctance to intervene, the state courts have justified judicial review of union discipline by three theories—a property theory, a contract theory, and a tort theory. The property theory posits that a member possesses property interests in his union;[3] the contract theory holds that a member contracts with the union when he joins, and the terms of the contract are the union's constitution and bylaws;[4] the tort theory suggests that a civil wrong is committed when a member's advantageous relationship with his union is disrupted.[5] Until federal preemption, state courts used these theories to intervene in the union discipline cases brought before them. Federal preemption, however, granted the National Labor Relations Board (NLRB) jurisdiction over such cases when they arguably involve unfair labor practices. The preemption doc-

---

[1] *See, e.g.,* People *ex rel.* Deverell v. Musical Mut. Protective Union, 118 N.Y. 101, 23 N.E. 129 (1889).

[2] Chafee, *The Internal Affairs of Associations Not for Profit,* 43 HARV. L. REV. 993 (1930).

[3] *See,* Summers, *Legal Limitations on Union Discipline,* 64 HARV. L. REV. 1049 (1951); and *The Law of Union Discipline: What the Courts Do in Fact,* 70 YALE L. J. 175 (1960), for discussion and criticism of the property theory.

[4] *See* Chapter V, *infra.*

[5] Cox, *Internal Affairs of Unions Under the Labor Reform Act of 1959,* 58 MICH. L. REV. 819, 835 (1960).

trine, therefore, limits the state courts' role in union discipline cases to examining the validity of rules dealing with purely internal union affairs. This chapter deals briefly with the preemption doctrine and the state courts' handling of internal union affairs.

The Preemption Doctrine

In *Amalgamated Association of Street Employees v. Lockridge*,[6] the Supreme Court had to determine when the National Labor Relations Board's jurisdiction preempts that of the state courts in union discipline cases. The Court reaffirmed its decision in *San Diego Building Trades Council v. Garmon*[7] which held that when an activity is arguably subject to the Board's jurisdiction, the states must defer to the exclusive competence of the Board. It limited its earlier holding in *International Association of Machinists v. Gonzales*[8] to those cases,

> ". . . focused on purely internal union matters," . . . a subject the National Labor Relations Act leaves principally to other processes of law.[9]

The state courts are allowed to act in those cases because the possibility of conflict with federal law is remote.[10]

The Court based its opinion on the need to avoid conflicting regulation of conduct by the Board and the states. It stated:

> The rationale for pre-emption, then, rests in large measure upon our determination that when it set down a federal labor policy Congress plainly meant to do more than simply alter the then-prevailing substantive law. It sought as well to restructure fundamentally the processes for effectuating that policy, deliberately placing the responsibility for applying and developing this comprehensive legal system in the hands of an expert administrative body rather than the federalized judicial system.[11]

The Court later argued that,

> [t]o leave the States free to regulate conduct so plainly within the central aim of federal regulation involves too great a danger of

---

[6] 403 U.S. 274, 77 L.R.R.M. 2501 (1971).

[7] 359 U.S. 236, 43 L.R.R.M. 2838 (1959).

[8] 356 U.S. 617, 42 L.R.R.M. 2135 (1958).

[9] 403 U.S. at 296, 77 L.R.R.M. at 2510.

[10] *Id.*, 77 L.R.R.M. at 2510.

[11] *Id.* at 288, 77 L.R.R.M. at 2507.

conflict between power asserted by Congress and requirements imposed by state law.[12]

Under *Lockridge,* if the union discipline is arguably an unfair labor practice, i.e., if the discipline somehow interferes with the members' job rights, the Board has exclusive jurisdiction over it; the state courts cannot intervene. For example, in *Lockridge* the Supreme Court refused to allow a state court to decide a case dealing with a union's procurement of a member's discharge from employment. The state courts examine only those union rules which concern internal union affairs and, therefore, are not subject to the National Labor Relations Act.[13] In other words, if the union discipline has caused a member to be discharged from his job, the NLRB will preempt the case. If, however, the discipline has caused a loss of membership in the union, that case will not be preempted. The provisions of the Landrum-Griffin Act do not preempt state courts from examining union discipline protected by Title I of that Act.[14]

Internal Union Rules

Although the Supreme Court's decision in *Lockridge* removed some substantive union rules from the reach of state courts, it left those rules dealing with purely internal matters within state court jurisdiction. Thus, discipline for financial offenses and, more important, discipline for political activities within the union are still subject to the review of state courts.

Generally, the courts have allowed unions latitude in disciplining members for financial offenses.[15] There appear to be no public policy reasons for disallowing such latitude. When a person joins a union, he knows he is incurring some basic financial obligations. Enforcing such obligations does not exact an undue hardship on the member. He can hardly plead ignorance of some financial obligation. Thus, the courts have allowed unions to discipline members for failure to pay initiation fees,[16]

---

[12] *Id.* at 291, 77 L.R.R.M. at 2508, *quoting from* San Diego Building Trades Council v. Garmon, 359 U.S. 236, 244, 43 L.R.R.M. 2838, 2841 (1959).

[13] 49 Stat. 449 (1935), *as amended,* 29 U.S.C. §§ 151 *et seq.* (1970).

[14] LMRDA § 103, 29 U.S.C. § 413 (1970), expressly provides that the Act's remedies are not exclusive.

[15] Summers, *The Law of Union Discipline: What the Courts Do in Fact,* 70 YALE L.J. 175, 188 (1960).

[16] *E.g.,* Seymour v. Essex County Printing Pressmen & Assistants' Union, 19 N.J. Misc. 665, 23 A.2d 169 (Sup. Ct. 1941).

dues,[17] or assessments [18] levied in accordance with the union's constitution.[19] The courts have allowed strict forfeitures of various union benefit payments even though the members have been guilty only of minor or temporary financial defaults.[20]

Traditionally, state courts have looked unfavorably upon union discipline for internal political activities. They have not normally granted relief on the grounds that political freedom within labor organizations is protected by public policy.[21] Instead, they have generally relied on some procedural defect in the disciplinary proceeding.[22] There has been, however, a trend toward developing a right to free speech and assembly for union members. Thus, in 1958, in *Madden v. Atkins*,[23] the New York Court of Appeals stated the following as public policy:

> . . . traditionally democratic means of improving their union may be freely availed of by members without fear of harm or penalty. And this necessarily includes the right to criticize current union leadership and, within the union, to oppose such leadership and its policies. . . . The price of free expression and of political opposition within a union can not be the risk of expulsion or other disciplinary action.[24]

Thus, the courts have begun to void rules which restrict the political freedom of members within their unions. These courts have come to recognize that rules prohibiting or severely limiting such freedom are contrary to public policy.

---

[17] *E.g.*, Brown v. Lehman, 141 Pa. Super. 467, 15 A.2d 513 (1940).

[18] *E.g.*, DeMille v. American Fed'n of Radio Artists, 31 Cal.2d 139, 187 P.2d 769, 21 L.R.R.M. 2111 (1947), *cert. denied*, 333 U.S. 876, 22 L.R.R.M. 2024 (1948).

[19] *See, e.g.*, Brown v. Hibbets, 290 N.Y. 559, 564, 49 N.E.2d 713, 716 (1943).

[20] *E.g.*, Hess v. Johnson, 41 App. Div. 465, 58 N.Y.S. 983 (2d Dep't 1899) ; Sammel v. Myrup, 12 N.Y.S.2d 217 (N.Y. Mun. Ct. 1939).

[21] Although in a great majority of cases the courts have given relief to members who have been disciplined for political activity within the union, they have not done so on the ground that this is a protected right. Summers, *Legal Limitations on Union Discipline*, 64 HARV. L. REV. 1049, 1069 (1951).

[22] *Id.* at 1070-71.

[23] 4 N.Y.2d 283, 174 N.Y.S.2d 633, 151 N.E.2d 73, 42 L.R.R.M. 2161 (1958).

[24] *Id.* at 293-94, 174 N.Y.S.2d at 640-41, 151 N.E.2d at 78, 42 L.R.R.M. at 2164.

CONCLUSION

Generally, the state courts have been reluctant to intervene in union discipline of members. They have recognized, however, that in some instances, justice requires that they intervene. Under the Supreme Court's decision in *Lockridge* the state courts have jurisdiction only over cases involving purely internal union matters. In the area of substantive union rules, this means that the state courts generally hear only cases involving financial or political offenses. In judging the cases involving substantive rules, the courts require that the rules not be contrary to public policy. If they are found to violate public policy, such rules are deemed void, and the union is not permitted to discipline a member for violating them. Rules regulating political activities within the union tend to be much more suspect than rules regulating financial obligations.

The primary justification which the state courts use to grant relief to members is that the union did not afford the member the proper procedural safeguards. Since the procedural rules of the union are purely internal, the state courts are able to intervene in this area. The courts generally require that for discipline to be valid, it must be for violation of a constitutional provision or bylaw, be imposed in the manner that the union constitution prescribes, and not be contrary to public policy. The state courts have developed fairly specific procedural rules which must be followed if a union is going to try properly a member.

The state courts pay lip service to the exhaustion doctrine, but they are willing to intervene whenever they feel that intervention is justified. They recognize that there are valid reasons for requiring a member to exhaust his internal union remedies, but they also are willing to ignore these reasons when they feel that it is appropriate.

CHAPTER III

The Federal Substantive Law

In 1935, Congress enacted the National Labor Relations Act [1] (Wagner Act) in order to protect employees who want to join or assist labor unions.[2] During the twelve years that followed, unions grew significantly in both size [3] and power.[4] As a result, in 1947, in order to curtail some of the ways in which unions were exercising their power, Congress again passed legislation in the field of labor law. It amended the Wagner Act by passing the Labor Management Relations Act [5] (Taft-Hartley Act) which, among other things, restricts union conduct by defining union unfair labor practices.[6]

In drafting the Taft-Hartley Act, Congress had to balance, on the one hand, the maintenance of employee freedom which lies at the heart of industrial democracy, and on the other hand, the right of a labor union to discipline its members so it can function effectively. As one authority on union discipline has stated, "These competing needs cannot be wholly reconciled." [7]

---

[1] 49 Stat. 449 (1935), *as amended*, 29 U.S.C. §§ 151 *et seq.* (1970).

[2] "The prime function of the [Wagner] Act was to protect employees against employer tactics designed either to obstruct organizational efforts or to withhold the fruits of those efforts." C. MORRIS, THE DEVELOPING LABOR LAW 28-29 (1971).

[3] "In 1935 only three million workers belonged to labor unions. In 1947 there were nearly fifteen million union members—roughly five times as many." A. COX & D. BOK, CASES AND MATERIALS ON LABOR LAW 105 (7th ed. 1969).

[4] "[T]he strongest unions . . . are the most powerful private economic organizations in the country." S. SLICHTER, THE CHALLENGE OF INDUSTRIAL RELATIONS 154 (1947).

[5] 61 Stat. 135 (1947), *as amended*, 29 U.S.C. §§ 141 *et seq.* (1970).

[6] NLRA § 8(b), 29 U.S.C. § 158(b) (1970) was added by the Taft-Hartley Act. It defines union unfair labor practices.

[7] Summers, *Union Democracy and Union Discipline*, N.Y.U. 5th CONF. ON LAB. 443, 459 (1952).

Congress attempted to guarantee employee freedom by amending Section 7 of the Wagner Act.[8] At the same time, Congress limited the power of a union to discipline its members by enacting Section 8(b)(1)(A).[9]

Section 7, which previously gave employees only the right to self-organize, to form, join, or assist labor unions, was amended also to give employees "the right to refrain from any or all such activities" except under certain collective bargaining contracts.[10]

Section 8(b)(1)(A) limits the action a union may take against a member by making it an unfair labor practice to restrain or coerce an employee in the exercise of his Section 7 rights. At the same time, the proviso in Section 8(b)(1)(A) makes it clear that the union may adopt internal rules on membership requirements.[11]

Professor Cox, upon examining Section 8(b)(1), made the following prediction:

> The scope and variety of the . . . problems suggest that Section 8(b)(1) may plunge the [National Labor Relations] Board into a dismal swamp of uncertainty. . . . A long period of uncertainty and heavy volume of litigation will be necessary before the questions of interpretation can be resolved.[12]

This prediction has proved to be accurate. Beginning in 1967, the Supreme Court has had to decide a series of cases dealing with union discipline and the meaning of Sections 7 and 8(b)

---

[8] 29 U.S.C. § 157 (1970).

[9] 29 U.S.C. § 158(b)(1)(A) (1970).

[10] Section 7 states:
Employees shall base the right to self-organization, to form, join, or assist labor organizations, to bargain collectively through representatives of their own choosing, and to engage in other concerted activities for the purpose of collective bargaining or other mutual aid or protection, and shall also have the right to refrain from any and all such activities except to the extent that such right may be affected by an agreement requiring membership in a labor organization as a condition of employment as authorized in Section 8(a)(3).

[11] Section 8(b)(1)(A) states:
It shall be an unfair labor practice for a labor organization or its agents (1) to restrain or coerce (A) employees in the exercise of the rights guaranteed in section 7: *Provided* that this paragraph shall not impair the right of a labor organization to prescribe its own rules with respect to the acquisition or retention of membership therein.

[12] Cox, *Some Aspects of the Labor Management Relations Act 1947*, 61 HARV. L. REV. 1, 33 (1947).

(1) (A) of the National Labor Relations Act. These decisions have answered some of the questions raised by these sections, given some guidance on how future cases should be decided, and left still other questions unresolved. This chapter will examine these cases and also the case law consisting of Board and circuit court decisions in an attempt to ascertain the present state of the substantive law of union discipline in this country.

THE KINDS OF ACTIVITIES FOR
WHICH A UNION MAY DISCIPLINE A MEMBER

On three occasions the Supreme Court examined union rules to decide whether they were enforceable against union members. This section will examine these three cases and then study how the Board and the circuit courts have applied the principles of these cases.

Allis-Chalmers

In 1967, the Supreme Court decided *NLRB v. Allis-Chalmers Manufacturing Co.*[13] This case posed the question of whether judicial enforcement of a reasonable fine against a full member of a union for crossing a properly authorized picket line to return to work during a strike is an unfair labor practice under Section 8(b) (1) (A). Does the fine represent an improper restraint on the rights of the members under Section 7 or does it represent a legitimate control device for the union?

The facts of the case have been concisely summarized by Justice Brennan:

> Employees at the West Allis, and La Crosse, Wisconsin, plants of respondent Allis-Chalmers Manufacturing Company were represented by locals of the United Automobile Workers. Lawful economic strikes were conducted at both plants in support of new contract demands. In compliance with the UAW constitution, the strikes were called with the approval of the International Union after at least two-thirds of the members of each local voted by secret ballot to strike. Some members of each local crossed the picket lines and worked during the strikes. After the strikes were over, the locals brought proceedings against these members charging them with violation of the International constitution and by-laws. The charges were heard by local trial committees in proceedings at which the charged members were represented by counsel. No claim of unfairness in the proceedings is made. The trials re-

---

[13] 388 U.S. 175, 65 L.R.R.M. 2449 (1967).

sulted in each charged member being found guilty of "conduct unbecoming a Union member" and being fined in a sum from $20 to
$100. Some of the fined members did not pay the fines and one of
the locals obtained a judgment in the amount of the fine against
one of its members, Benjamin Natzke, in a test suit brought in
the Milwaukee County Court.[14]

Using these facts, Allis-Chalmers filed a charge with the Board
alleging that the union was violating Section 8(b)(1)(A). The
trial examiner recommended that the complaint be dismissed,
and the Board, relying on the proviso in Section 8(b)(1)(A),
agreed.[15] A panel of the Seventh Circuit Court of Appeals also
agreed,[16] but on rehearing, that court, sitting en banc, reversed
and remanded the decision to the Board.[17] The Supreme Court
then sustained the Board's original action in a five to four decision that required a separate, concurring opinion to establish the
majority.

Justice Brennan, joined by three other justices, wrote the
majority opinion. Justice White provided the fifth vote needed
for dismissal of the complaint but indicated that he was "doubt-
ful about the implications of some of [the decision's] generalized
statements." [18]

The Seventh Circuit read Section 8(b)(1)(A) literally and
held that a union may only discipline its members by explusion.[19]
It found that:

> The statutes in question present no ambiguities whatsoever, and
> therefore do not require recourse to legislative history for clari-
> fication.[20]

Justice Brennan disagreed. He found that the phrase "restrain
or coerce" is vague, and he therefore resorted to the legislative
history of the Act to see what the phrase means. In doing so,
the majority admonished,

---

[14] *Id.* at 177, 65 L.R.R.M. at 2449.

[15] Local 248, UAW (Allis-Chalmers Mfg. Co.), 149 N.L.R.B. 67, 57 L.R.R.M.
1242 (1964). Member Leedom dissented.

[16] Allis-Chalmers Mfg. Co. v. NLRB, 60 L.R.R.M. 2097 (7th Cir. 1965).

[17] Allis-Chalmers Mfg. Co. v. NLRB, 358 F.2d 656, 61 L.R.R.M. 2498 (7th
Cir. 1966).

[18] 388 U.S. at 199, 65 L.R.R.M. at 2458.

[19] 358 F.2d at 659, 61 L.R.R.M. at 2500.

[20] *Id.* at 660, 61 L.R.R.M. at 2500.

. . . that labor legislation is peculiarly the product of legislative compromise of strongly held views, *Local 1976, Carpenters' Union v. Labor Board*, 357 U.S. 93, 99-100, and that legislative history may not be disregarded merely because it is arguable that a provision may unambiguously embrace conduct called in question. *National Woodwork Mfgs. Assn. v. NLRB*, 386 U.S. 612, 619-620.[21]

By resorting to the legislative history, Justice Brennan concluded that Congress did not mean to limit the power of unions to regulate their internal affairs. He stated:

. . . there are a number of assurances by its sponsors that [Section 8(b)(1)(A)] was not meant to regulate the internal affairs of unions.[22]

He quoted several passages that support this viewpoint.[23] He also quoted Professor Summers:

The economic strike against the employer is the ultimate weapon in labor's arsenal for achieving agreement upon its terms, and "[t]he power to fine or expel strikebreakers is essential if the union is to be an effective bargaining agent." [24]

Justice Brennan also concluded that Congress did not intend to remove labor's cherished power to conduct an effective strike. In addition, he argued that, for policy reasons, the same re-

---

[21] 388 U.S. at 179, 65 L.R.R.M. at 2450.

[22] *Id.* at 186, 65 L.R.R.M. at 2453.

[23] The majority quoted Senator Taft's answer to Senator Pepper's objection that Section 8(b)(2) would interfere in the internal affairs of unions.

The pending measure does not propose any limitation with respect to the internal affairs of unions. They still will be able to fire any members they wish to fire, *and they still will be able to try any of their members.* All that they will not be able to do . . . is this: if they fine a member for some reason other than nonpayment of dues they cannot make his employer discharge him from his job and throw him out of work. That is the only result of the provision under discussion. [93 Cong. Rec. 4193, II Leg. Hist. 1097] (Emphasis supplied by the Court.)

The Court observed that this statement was made while Section 8(b)(1)(A) was also under consideration and "is therefore significant evidence against reading § 8(b)(1)(A) as contemplating regulation of internal discipline." *Id.* at 185, 65 L.R.R.M. at 2453.

The Court also quoted Senator Ball:

It was never the intention of the sponsors of the pending amendment to interfere with the internal affairs or organization of unions. [93 Cong. Rec. 4272, II Leg. Hist. 1141.] (Emphasis supplied by the Court.)

Id. at 187, 65 L.R.R.M. at 2453.

[24] *Id.* at 181, 65 L.R.R.M. at 2451.

sults must be reached when effecting union discipline. If a union is strong, then fining a member is a lesser punishment than expelling him; therefore, it should be acceptable. If a union is weak, expulsion may be too small a punishment to maintain order. Therefore, if a weak union is to be effective, it must be able to use a means of discipline other than expulsion. Fines meet this need.[25] Justice Brennan decided that, based on the Act's legislative history and on policy considerations, a union may impose a reasonable fine on members for crossing a picket line.

The Court found, absent a showing to the contrary, that the members fined had full union membership.[26] As a result, it concluded:

> Whether [an unfair labor practice would be found] if the locals had imposed fines on members whose membership was in fact limited to the obligation of paying monthly dues is a question not before us and upon which we intimate no view.[27]

The Court did not consider the effect of the size of the fines.

The majority concluded that if the fine itself is legitimate, then there is no question of its enforceability in court. Since the relationship between a member and the union is viewed as contractual, the contractual obligations are enforceable in court.[28] To show that this is not a recent innovation, the Court cited an 1867 case, *Master Stevedores' Association v. Walsh*,[29] in which a fine was enforced by a court.[30]

Having held that the fine was not restraint or coercion and was enforceable in court, Justice Brennan did not need to use the proviso in Section 8(b)(1)(A), as the Board had, to justify his holding. He did, however, indicate that he felt it lent "cogent support" to his conclusions.[31]

Justice White, in his concurring opinion, said that he found the majority opinion more persuasive than the minority and

---

25 *Id.* at 183, 65 L.R.R.M. at 2452.

26 *Id.* at 196, 65 L.R.R.M. at 2457.

27 *Id.* at 197, 65 L.R.R.M. at 2457.

28 *Id.* at 182, 65 L.R.R.M. at 2452.

29 2 Daly 1 (N.Y. 1867).

30 388 U.S. at 182, 65 L.R.R.M. at 2451.

31 *Id.* at 191, 65 L.R.R.M. at 2455.

therefore joined it. He opined that future cases would have to be decided on a case-by-case basis since,

> . . . [not] every conceivable internal union rule which impinges upon the § 7 rights of union members is valid and enforceable by expulsion and court action.[32]

Justice Black wrote a strong dissenting opinion and was joined by Justices Douglas, Harlan, and Stewart. They found, as did the Seventh Circuit, that the words "restrain or coerce" are clear, not vague.[33] Even if they were not so, Justice Black found support in the legislative history for his view of this literal interpretation.[34] He also pointed out that the proviso cannot justify the Court's holding since, as the Court recognized, a fine may be more coercive than expulsion.[35]

The minority then proceeded to criticize other parts of the Court's opinion. Justice Black emphasized that the contract theory is legal fiction:[36] under traditional contract law, the fine would be unenforceable.[37]

Finally, Justice Black pointed out that the implied dichotomy between full union members and those who simply pay dues is often useless. The average employee will not be aware that he has a choice nor will he be aware of the consequences of his choice.[38]

Although the legislative history seems to support Justice Brennan's construction of the phrase "restrain or coerce," an examination reveals that there is relatively little history extant on this

---

[32] *Id.* at 198, 65 L.R.R.M. at 2548.

[33] *Id.* at 201, 65 L.R.R.M. at 2459.

[34] Justice Black quoted Senator Taft on the effect of Section 8(b)(1)(A) on strikes.

> "I can see nothing in the pending measure which . . . would in some way outlaw strikes. It would outlaw threats against employees. It would not outlaw anybody striking who wanted to strike. It would not prevent anyone using the strike in a legitimate way . . . . All it would do would be to outlaw such restraint and coercion as would prevent people from going to work if they wished to go to work." 93 Cong. Rec. 4436, II Leg. Hist. 1207.

Id. at 202 n. 1, 65 L.R.R.M. at 2459 n. 1.

[35] *Id.* at 204, 65 L.R.R.M. at 2460.

[36] *Id.* at 207, 65 L.R.R.M. at 2461.

[37] *Id.* at 208, 65 L.R.R.M. at 2462.

[38] *Id.* at 215, 65 L.R.R.M. at 2465.

section.[39] What history is available does support the interpretation given the phrase by Justice Brennan. The quotations he used in his opinion show that Congress did not intend to regulate the internal affairs of unions. Justice Black, in reaching his opposite conclusion, relied on a statement by Senator Taft. As the majority pointed out,

> . . . any inference that Senator Taft envisioned that § 8(b)(1)(A) intruded into and regulated internal union affairs is negated by his categorical statements to the contrary in the contemporaneous debates on § 8(b)(2).[40]

In light of this and the statements of Senator Ball and others to the effect that the section was not intended to regulate internal union affairs, one must conclude that the legislative history, scant as it is, offers more support to Justice Brennan's position than to Justice Black's.

Setting aside for a moment the question of court enforcement of fines, the proviso in Section 8(b)(1)(A) justifies fines enforceable by expulsion. Under the proviso, expulsion is an acceptable means of discipline.[41] If a fine were enforceable only by expulsion, the member would be able to determine for himself which punishment was more coercive. He would never be subject to discipline harsher than expulsion—a permissible punishment. Apparently both the legislative history and the proviso indicate that Section 8(b)(1)(A) should not be interpreted as prohibiting a union from fining its members.

Although the Court appears justified in holding the fines proper, the minority persuasively concluded that court enforcement should not be allowed. The Court's reliance on the contract theory seems to be improper because a contract has never been shown to exist.[42] In order to make a contract both parties

---

[39] Section 8(b)(1)(A) was not included in the original Senate bill as it came from the Committee on Labor and Public Welfare. It was added as an amendment on the Senate floor, and it was later adopted by the conference committee without change. Therefore, there were no House debates or committee reports, and the Senate debate was brief.

[40] 388 U.S. at 189-190, 65 L.R.R.M. at 2455.

[41] As Justice White said in his concurring opinion in *Allis-Chalmers*: "[N]either the majority nor the dissent in this case questions . . . the propriety of expulsion to enforce the rule."
Id. at 198, 65 L.R.R.M. at 2458.

[42] As the minority pointed out, quoting Professor Summers, the majority's own expert,

> The contract of membership is . . . a legal fabrication . . . . What are the terms of the contract? The constitutional provisions, particularly

must intend to make one or act in a way that indicates they intend to be bound, or in a way to lead a court to decide they are "deemed to be bound."

Also, a contract must consist of definite terms.[43] In *Allis-Chalmers*, the members were charged with "conduct unbecoming a Union member." Such a phrase may be considered too indefinite to be enforceable as a contract term. As Professor Summers noted, many union constitutions contain disciplinary provisions so vague as to fall short of the certainty ordinarily required in a contract.[44]

Voluntary consent is needed to form a contract.[45] An employee who joins because the union has negotiated a union shop contract may believe he must join the union in order to retain his job.[46] Members acting under such belief are not giving their voluntary consent to join.

---

those governing discipline, are so notoriously vague that they fall far short of the certainty ordinarily required of a contract. The member has no choice as to terms but is compelled to adhere to the inflexible ones presented. Even then, the union is not bound, for it retains the unlimited power to amend any term at any time. . . . In short, membership is a special relationship. It is as far removed from the main channel of contract law as the relationships created by marriage. . . .
Id. at 207 n. 6, 65 L.R.R.M. at 2461 n. 6.

[43] RESTATEMENT OF CONTRACTS § 32 (1932); 1 WILLISTON ON CONTRACTS § 37 (3d ed. 1957); 1 CORBIN ON CONTRACTS § 95 (1963).

[44] Summers, *Legal Limitations on Union Discipline*, 64 HARV. L. REV. 1049, 1055 (1951). *E.g.*, the *Constitution of the International Ladies' Garment Workers' Union*, Art. 20, § 1(i) and (l) (1971) provides:

Section 1. Discipline of members.
A member may be censured, fined, suspended, expelled or otherwise disciplined. . .
(i) for any action or conduct detrimental to the interests of the I.L.G.W.U. or a subordinate organization; . . .
(l) for any action or conduct unbecoming to a member which occurs in connection with his membership in the I.L.G.W.U. or employment in its jurisdiction; . . .
The Constitution and By-Laws, Amalgamated Clothing Workers of America, Art. XI, § 1(b) (1974) provides:
(b) Any member shall be subject to discipline who is found guilty, after notice of and opportunity for hearing upon charges, of violating any provision of this Constitution and By-Laws or a decision of the General Executive Board, or of the local union or joint board, or dishonesty, misconduct, denial of the privileges of membership to any other member or conduct detrimental to the welfare of the Amalgamated.

[45] Baker v. Morton, 79 U.S. 150 (1870).

[46] *See* Union Starch & Refining Co., 87 N.L.R.B. No. 137, 25 L.R.R.M. 1176 (1949), *enforced,* 186 F.2d 1008, 27 L.R.R.M. 2342 (7th Cir. 1951),

Traditionally, courts have used the contract theory to strike down union discipline.[47] It has not been used to enforce union fines. The *Master Stevedores' Association v. Walsh* case cited by the majority in *Allis-Chalmers* is exceptional.[48] Courts in other states have rejected court enforcement of fines unless such fines were specifically provided for in the union's constitution or bylaws.[49] The first case to use a contract theory to hold a fine enforceable in court without such a contract clause was decided in 1958.[50] Given the contract theory background and the unions' traditional distrust of the courts, Congress probably did not even seriously consider the possibility of fines being enforced in court. Since the contract theory is not valid, the Congressional purpose in passing the Taft-Hartley Act must be considered to ascertain whether the fines should be enforceable in court. The Congressional purpose was to allow the individual a choice, and since Congress did forbid other external means of enforcement,[51] it seems reasonable to conclude that Congress did not intend union fines to be court-enforceable. Unfortunately, unless the Court reconsiders the issue, the unions now have the right to seek court enforcement of their fines.[52]

---

cert. denied, 342 U.S. 815, 28 L.R.R.M. 2625 (1951), in which it was held that an employee may be required by the collective bargaining agreement to pay the union an initiation fee and periodic dues, but he may not be required to join the union.

[47] Summers, *supra* note 44, at 1051.

[48] In that case, court enforcement was provided for in a bylaw. New York does not, in the absence of such a bylaw, permit a voluntary association to enforce such fines in court. Merchants' Ladies Garment Ass'n v. Coat House of William M. Schwartz, Inc., 152 Misc. 130, 273 N.Y.S. 317 (N.Y. Mun. Ct. 1934).

[49] Retail Clerks Local 629 v. Christiansen, 67 Wash.2d 29, 60 L.R.R.M. 2389 (1965); United Glass Workers' Local 188 v. Seitz, 65 Wash.2d 640, 58 L.R.R.M. 2543 (1965).

[50] Local 756, UAW v. Woychik, 5 Wis.2d 528, 93 N.W.2d 336, 43 L.R.R.M. 2741 (1958).

[51] NLRA § 8(b)(2), 29 U.S.C. § 158(b)(2) (1970) forbids a union to attempt to cause an employer to discharge an employee for any reason other than for not tendering required dues and initiation fees.

[52] The General Counsel and Assistant General Counsel of the UAW wrote an article in which they pointed out:

> An anomalous aside to the *Allis-Chalmers* . . . case is that the International Executive Board of the UAW has decided that, as a matter of policy, the International Union, UAW, will not seek to collect disciplinary fines in court. Further, that it will discourage UAW locals

After the Court's decision in *Allis-Chalmers,* it decided two other cases relating to acceptable vis-à-vis unacceptable discipline. These two decisions have helped to clarify and modify the Court's decision in *Allis-Chalmers.*

Marine Workers

The year after *Allis-Chalmers* was decided, the Supreme Court considered another case in the area of employee rights versus union disciplinary needs. In *NLRB v. Industrial Union of Marine Workers,*[53] the Court considered whether a union could expel a member for filing a charge against it with the Board without first exhausting his internal remedies. Does the member have the right to go to the Board whenever he has been the victim of an unfair labor practice, or may a union require its members to allow it to resolve such a charge internally, if possible?

The facts of the case can be summarized as follows. A union member brought suit against his local president alleging that the officer had violated the union's constitution. The local heard the charges and exonerated the president. Without exhausting his internal union remedies as the union constitution required, the member then filed a charge with the Board. The union expelled him for filing the charge in violation of the union's constitution. He then filed a second charge with the Board alleging a Section 8(b)(1)(A) violation based on his expulsion. The Board issued a remedial order,[54] but the Third Circuit refused to enforce it.[55]

In an eight-to-one decision, with Justice Douglas writing for the majority, the Court found that free, unimpeded access to the Board is necessary. Justice Douglas pointed out that under the Court's decision in *Allis-Chalmers,* ". . . § 8(b)(1)(A)

---

from doing so, and that the International Union will not lend financial support to locals which so act.

Schlossberg & Lubin, *Union Democracy and Union Discipline,* N.Y.U. 23d CONF. ON LAB. 207, 218 n. 42 (1970).

[53] 391 U.S. 418, 68 L.R.R.M. 2257 (1968).

[54] Industrial Union of Marine Workers v. NLRB, 159 N.L.R.B. 1065, 62 L.R.R.M. 1301 (1966).

[55] Industrial Union of Marine Workers v. NLRB, 379 F.2d 702, 65 L.R.R.M. 2629 (3d Cir. 1967).

assures a union freedom of self-regulation where its legitimate internal affairs are concerned."

He went on to say,

> [b]ut where a union rule penalizes a member for filing an unfair labor practice charge with the Board, other considerations of public policy come into play.[56]

Since a charge must be filed within six months of the commission of the unfair labor practice alleged,[57] and since the Board cannot initiate its own proceedings, the Board must rely,

> "upon the initiative of individual persons." *Nash v. Florida Industrial Comm'n*, 389 U.S. 235, 238. The policy of keeping people "completely free from coercion," *ibid.*, against making complaints to the Board is therefore important in the functioning of the Act as an organic whole.[58]

Based on these considerations, Justice Douglas concluded:

> Any coercion used to discourage, retard, or defeat that access [to the Board] is beyond the legitimate interests of a labor organization.[59]

The Court also held that the proviso in Section 101(a)(4) of the Labor Management Reporting and Disclosure Act of 1959 [60] (Landrum-Griffin Act) granted the courts use of their discretion rather than granting the unions power to restrict union members' conduct.[61]

This case modified the Court's earlier holding in *Allis-Chalmers*. There, Justice Brennan and the three justices who joined him in his opinion seemed to hold that a union may discipline a member for any internal matter. In *Marine Workers*, the Court

---

[56] 391 U.S. 424, 68 L.R.R.M. 2259.

[57] NLRA § 10(b), 29 U.S.C. § 160(b) (1970).

[58] 391 U.S. 424, 68 L.R.R.M. 2259.

[59] *Id.*, 68 L.R.R.M. at 2259.

[60] 29 U.S.C. § 411(a)(4) (1970) states:

> No labor organization shall limit the right of any member thereof to institute an action in any court, or in a proceeding before any administrative agency . . . *Provided*, That any such member may be required to exhaust reasonable hearing procedures (but not to exceed a four-month lapse of time) within such organization, before instituting legal or administrative proceedings. . . .

See the discussion on exhaustion in Chapter IV, *infra*.

[61] 391 U.S. at 426, 68 L.R.R.M. at 2260.

makes clear that Justice White was correct in *Allis-Chalmers* when he indicated that not all such discipline is permissible. If the discipline is contrary to public policy, it is not allowable.

Scofield

In 1969, for the third time in three years, a case concerning union discipline reached the Supreme Court. In *Scofield v. NLRB*,[62] the Court was called upon to decide whether a union could legitimately impose fines on members for violating a union rule concerning production and pay ceilings. Does a member have the right to earn as much as he can by his efforts, or may a union limit the amount a member may earn per day in order to serve legitimate union goals?

The facts of the case are as follows. The petitioners were members of the UAW and were employed by the Wisconsin Motor Corporation. They were paid on a piecework basis. The union, since 1938, had set a ceiling on the wages a member could earn each day by exceeding the machine rate. If a member's daily piecework earnings exceeded the ceiling, the excess was "banked" by the company for a time when the member did not exceed the ceiling. Since 1944, a member who violated the rule had been subject to fines and expulsion. The fine for each offense was one dollar, but repeat offenders could be fined up to one hundred dollars for "conduct unbecoming a union member." The union and employer had bargained over the ceiling level, but the contract did not forbid the employer from paying employees for work performed which exceeded that level. In 1961, the petitioners, among other union members, were found to have demanded and received immediate payment for work beyond the ceiling. They were fined fifty to one hundred dollars and suspended from the union. When the petitioners refused to pay the fines, the union brought an action in state court for their collection. The petitioners then filed a charge with the Board alleging a violation of Section 8(b)(1) (A). In a split decision, the Board found no unfair labor practice and dismissed the complaint.[63] The Seventh Circuit affirmed the Board's decision.[64]

---

[62] 394 U.S. 423, 70 L.R.R.M. 3105 (1969).

[63] Local 283, UAW (Wisconsin Motor Corp.), 145 N.L.R.B. 1097, 55 L.R.R.M. 1085 (1964).

[64] Scofield v. NLRB, 393 F.2d 49, 67 L.R.R.M. 2673 (7th Cir. 1968).

When the case reached the Supreme Court, the decision of the Board and the Seventh Circuit was affirmed in a seven to one decision. Justice White, who was the swing vote in *Allis-Chalmers,* delivered the majority opinion this time. Citing his dissent in *Allis-Chalmers,* Justice Black was the lone dissenter.

The Court held that the rule restricting daily earnings was one that served legitimate union interests and was not contrary to any public policy. As such, it was valid and could be enforced against members by court-enforceable fines. The Court said:

> . . . § 8(b)(1) leaves a union free to enforce a properly adopted rule which reflects a legitimate union interest, impairs no policy Congress has imbedded in the labor laws, and is reasonably enforced against union members who are free to leave the union and escape the rule.[65]

This is apparently the approach to be used in the future to ascertain the propriety of the union discipline.

In *Scofield,* the Court found that the rule reflected a legitimate union interest. It quoted the trial examiner who said that such unity of action was "manifestly a matter of affecting the interest of the group . . ." and was important to its collective bargaining strength.[66] The Court noted that production ceilings have long been recognized as legitimate union goals for the purpose of mitigating possible adverse consequences of unlimited piecework pay systems.[67]

The petitioners asserted that the union action here contravened various statutory policies. The Court ruled, however, that the union regulation did not impede any statutory policy and therefore affirmed the Seventh Circuit's decision.[68]

Once again, the Court did not fully explore the major problems with these fines—court enforcement. It did, however, give broad guidelines to help determine the legality of the discipline. Justice White's summary synthesizes the holdings of the three cases.

---

[65] 394 U.S. at 430, 70 L.R.R.M. at 3108.

[66] *Id.* at 425, 70 L.R.R.M. at 3106.

[67] *Id.* at 431, 70 L.R.R.M. at 3108.

[68] *Id.* at 436, 70 L.R.R.M. at 3110.

What Rules Are Proper?

The Supreme Court's decisions in *Allis-Chalmers, Marine Workers,* and *Scofield,* taken together, have provided general guidelines on activities for which a member may be disciplined. The member must have violated a union rule designed to serve legitimate union interests. The rule must also be consistent with general public policy.

In general, a rule reflects a legitimate union interest if it furthers (or prevents hindrance of) the union in fulfilling its duty as the exclusive bargaining agent of those it represents. An example of such a rule forbids members from crossing picket lines of a sister union [69] or of their own union, as in *Allis-Chalmers.* This is justified on the grounds that unions use strikes as their ultimate weapon in the collective bargaining process and that solidarity is deemed essential for the union. Likewise, rules against working for wages below union scale, participating in wildcat strikes, or failing to meet financial obligations have all been held valid. [70]

The union rule must not be contrary to public policy. There are five areas in which the Board and the courts have found union discipline improper for violating public policy.

First, it has been established that a union may not restrict a member's access to the Board or the courts. As was discussed earlier, [71] *Marine Workers* held that a union member may not be expelled from a union for filing an unfair labor practice charge against it with the Board. The Board has held that, for the same reasons, a member may not be fined for such conduct. [72] Likewise, the Board and courts have extended this protection to a member who encourages another to file such a charge. [73] In addition, a member who files a lawsuit against the union is not subject to union discipline for having done so. [74]

---

[69] American Newspaper Guild, Local 35 (Washington Post Co.), 186 N.L.R.B. No. 133, 75 L.R.R.M. 1438 (1970).

[70] *See* Summers, *supra* note 44, at 1063-72.

[71] *See* note 53, *supra,* and the accompanying text.

[72] Local 138, Operating Engineers (Skura), 148 N.L.R.B. 679, 57 L.R.R.M. 1009 (1964).

[73] Philadelphia Moving Pictures Machine Operators, Local 307, 159 N.L.R.B. No. 124, 62 L.R.R.M. 1315 (1966), *enforced,* 382 F.2d 598, 65 L.R.R.M. 3020 (3d Cir. 1967).

[74] Operating Engineers, Local 3 v. Burroughs, 417 F.2d 370, 72 L.R.R.M. 2577 (9th Cir. 1969).

The union is deemed to have no legitimate interest in punishing those who have a grievance against it.

This general rule, however, is subject to an exception. A member who circulates [75] or files [76] a decertification petition with the Board may be suspended or expelled for such activity. The reason is that, by making such action, the member is threatening the very existence of the union. The union, according to this rationale, therefore has the right to defend itself. By expelling the member, the union excludes him from meetings at which the union's strategy may be planned. Thus, the expulsion is serving a legitimate union function. Although the member may be expelled for such action, he may not be fined.[77]

There are two reasons for which expulsion is acceptable while the fine is not. First, whereas explusion serves the legitimate purpose of purging the union of "traitors," fining serves no legitimate purpose. Its sole function is punitive. Second, if a member is attempting to cause his union to be decertified, his membership is probably of little value to him. Therefore, the deterrent effect of the threat of a fine, rather than expulsion, would probably be greater for a member considering filing a decertification petition. For similar reasons, a member who solicits authorization cards in support of a rival union may be expelled, but he may not be fined.[78]

If the member attacking the union in this manner is an officer of the union, he may be removed from office for his actions.[79] Again, this is a legitimate defensive measure. A member attempting to scuttle the union should not be allowed to be in a position of leadership in it.

---

[75] United Lodge 66, IAM (Smith-Lee Co.) 182 N.L.R.B. No. 129, 74 L.R.R.M. 1201 (1970) (by implication).

[76] Price v. NLRB, 373 F.2d 443, 64 L.R.R.M. 2495 (9th Cir. 1967), *cert. denied*, 392 U.S. 904, 68 L.R.R.M. 2408 (1968), *enforcing* 154 N.L.R.B. 692, 60 L.R.R.M. 1008 (1965); Tawas Tube Products, Inc., 151 N.L.R.B. 46, 58 L.R.R.M. 1330 (1965).

[77] International Molders, Local 125 (Blackhawk Tanning Co.) 178 N.L.R.B. No. 25, 72 L.R.R.M. 1049 (1969), *enforced*, 442 F.2d 92, 77 L.R.R.M. 2067 (7th Cir. 1971).

[78] Tri-Rivers Marine Engineers Union (U.S. Steel Corp.), 189 N.L.R.B. No. 108, 77 L.R.R.M. 1027 (1971).

[79] United Lodge 66, IAM (Smith-Lee Co.) 182 N.L.R.B. No. 129, 74 L.R.R.M. 1201 (1970).

A second area in which union discipline is improper is in performance of civic duties. The Board has held that a union member may not be disciplined for testifying at an administrative [80] or arbitration hearing.[81] The union is deemed to have no legitimate interest in silencing testimony. Any attempt to compel such silence would be contrary to the public good. This would also include areas such as testifying before Congress and reporting violations of the law.

A third area in which union discipline is illegal is where such discipline is in violation of, or would encourage violation of other sections of the Act. For example, a union may not discipline a supervisory worker for his actions as management's representative in adjusting grievances and collective bargaining since the effect might be in violation of Section 8(b)(1)(B) of the Act.[82] Likewise, a member may not be disciplined for accepting a temporary promotion to a supervisory position.[83] Similarly, a union may not discipline its members for working behind a picket line that is in violation of Section 8(b)(4)(i)(ii)(B).[84] To allow any disciplinary action would be to allow unions to punish members for upholding the law.

The fourth area in which public policy overrides union interests arises where a union may not discipline a member for refusing to violate the collective bargaining contract. In *Scofield,* the Supreme Court rejected the contention that the union's rule had effected such discipline. It did, however, suggest that if it had, the rule would have been unenforceable.[85] The Board and the courts have applied this to *Painters, District Council 9,* in which the union attempted to rule unilaterally to restrict the workers' output to a production level below

---

[80] Automotive Salesmen's Ass'n (Spitler-Demmer, Inc.), 184 N.L.R.B. No. 64, 74 L.R.R.M. 1576 (1970).

[81] Teamsters, Local 788 (San Juan Islands Cannery), 190 N.L.R.B. No. 5, 77 L.R.R.M. 1458 (1971).

[82] Florida Power & Light Co. v. IBEW Local 641, 417 U.S. 790, 86 L.R.R.M. 2689 (1974).

[83] Teamsters, Local 633 (Continental Oil Co.), 193 N.L.R.B. No. 84, 78 L.R.R.M. 1424 (1971).

[84] Local 18, Operating Engineers (B.D. Morgan & Co.) 205 N.L.R.B. No. 75, 84 L.R.R.M. 1319 (1973).

[85] 394 U.S. at 433, 70 L.R.R.M. at 3109.

that agreed upon in the collective bargaining pact. This was found to be an unenforceable rule.[86]

This case was distinguishable from *Scofield* on two grounds. First, in *Scofield*, the employer acquiesced and cooperated in the implementation and application of the rule. Second, the quota the union imposed in *Scofield* was above, rather than below, the production level of the average efficient worker. By setting a production level below the bargained one, the union was improperly altering the collective bargaining agreement. The Board has also applied this principle to the case of a member who crosses a picket line when the collective bargaining agreement contains a provision that there be no suspension of work during the life of the contract. The union may not discipline the member whether the picket line is its own [87] or another union's.[88]

The fifth area in which there are restrictions on a union's right to discipline members is the area of political activities. These activities may be either outside or inside the union. The union is deemed to have no legitimate interest in restricting a member's outside political activities.[89] He should be able to work for the party, policies, and candidates that he desires. For example, one state court has ruled that where a member attempted to secure a state right-to-work law, he was immune from discipline.[90] The Landrum-Griffin Act guarantees the rights of free speech and assembly within the union.[91] A union member

---

[86] Painters, District Council 9 v. NLRB, 453 F.2d 783, 79 L.R.R.M. 2145 (2d Cir. 1971), *cert. denied*, 408 U.S. 930, 80 L.R.R.M. 2855 (1972), *enforcing* 186 N.L.R.B. No. 140, 75 L.R.R.M. 1465 (1970)

[87] Glaziers, Local 1162 (Tusco Glass, Inc.), 177 N.L.R.B. No. 37, 73 L.R.R.M. 1125 (1969).

[88] Communications Workers, Local 1197 (Western Electric Co.), 202 N.L.R.B. No. 45, 82 L.R.R.M. 1530 (1973); Local 12419, UMW (National Grinding Wheel Co.), 176 N.L.R.B. No. 89, 71 L.R.R.M. 1311 (1969).

[89] *See* Summers, *supra* note 44, at 1068-69.

[90] Mitchell v. IAM, 16 Cal. Rpt. 813, 49 L.R.R.M. 2116 (Dist. Ct. App. 1961).

[91] LMRDA § 101(a)(2); 29 U.S.C. § 411(a)(2) (1970):

> Every member of any labor organization shall have the right to meet and assemble freely with other members; and to express any views, arguments, or opinions; and to express at meetings of the labor organization his views, upon candidates in the election of the labor organization or upon any business properly before the meeting, subject to the organization's established and reasonable rules pertaining to the conduct of meetings: *Provided*, That nothing herein shall be construed to impair

may meet with other members [92] and oppose union policies [93] or candidates [94] without being subject to discipline.

In sum, for discipline to be proper, it must be for violation of a rule that the union has a legitimate interest in enforcing. Generally, such a rule promotes the union's ability to serve as the exclusive bargaining agent of those it represents. The rule must also be one that is not contrary to public policy. Even if a union has a legitimate reason for punishing a member, it may not do so if its real motive is to discipline him for an improper purpose.[95] The Board and the courts have found that a union may not discipline a member for utilizing the Board or the courts, or for performing his civic duties; neither may it require him to violate the law or a contract, nor limit his speech and assembly rights. In all of these areas, public policy overrides whatever interest the union may have.

MEMBERSHIP

A union may take direct disciplinary action only against its members.[96] Exactly what constitutes membership, however, is not

> the right of a labor organization to adopt and enforce reasonable rules as to the responsibility of every member toward the organization as an institution and to his refraining from conduct that would interfere with its performance of its legal or contractual obligations.

[92] Kuebler v. Lithographers, Local 24-P, 473 F.2d 359, 82 L.R.R.M. 2717 (6th Cir. 1973).

[93] Cole v. Hall, 462 F.2d 777, 80 L.R.R.M. 3000 (2d Cir. 1972).

[94] Retail Clerks, Local 648 v. Retail Clerks International Ass'n, 299 F. Supp. 1012, 70 L.R.R.M. 3366 (D.D.C. 1969).

[95] NLRB v. Local 294, Teamsters, 470 F.2d 57, 81 L.R.R.M. 2920 (2d Cir. 1972), *enforcing* 193 N.L.R.B. No. 138, 78 L.R.R.M. 1479 (1971); Carpenters, Local 22 (Graziano Const. Co.), 195 N.L.R.B. No. 5, 79 L.R.R.M. 1194 (1972); Automotive Salesmen's Ass'n (Spitler-Demmer, Inc.), 184 N.L.R.B. No. 64, 74 L.R.R.M. 1576 (1970).

[96] NLRB v. Granite State Joint Board, Textile Workers, Local 1029, 409 U.S. 213, 81 L.R.R.M. 2853 (1972). A union can, in many circumstances, interfere with the job rights of nonmembers by requesting the employer to impose discipline for improper work-related conduct. However, if a former member violates union rules after he resigns, the union may expel him, Pattern Makers' Ass'n (Lietzau Pattern Co.), 199 N.L.R.B. No. 14, 81 L.R.R.M. 1177 (1972), or impose a fine upon him if it is enforceable only by expulsion, Local 1255, IAM v. NLRB, 456 F.2d 1214, 79 L.R.R.M. 2787 (5th Cir. 1972). Since the employee is not in the union, the expulsion is not deemed to be discipline. The proviso in Section 8(b)(1)(A) is viewed as protecting the union's right to expel a member or deny readmission to an ex-member for not paying a fine.

clear. When an employee should be considered a member, what constitutes resignation, when resignation is effective, and what limits a union may place on a member's right to resign are examined in this section.

What Constitutes Membership?

In *Allis-Chalmers,* the Supreme Court asserted that the employees were full members of the union. It did not consider the resulting decision had they not been members. This raises two interesting questions. First, at what point does a nonmember become a member? Second, is this distinction meaningful to the employees who are faced with choosing between membership and nonmembership?

If there is no requirement in the collective bargaining agreement that an employee be a member of the union, then if he is paying dues, it is reasonable to assume that he is voluntarily a full member. The problem occurs when an employee is required by the collective bargaining agreement to pay an initiation fee and monthly dues. He may be required to pay them even if he is not a member of the union.[97] Since the union, as the exclusive bargaining agent of the employees, must bargain for all the members of the bargaining unit, both union members and nonmembers, Congress has allowed the unions to bargain for a requirement that all employees pay initiation fees and dues except where state law specifies otherwise. The rationale therein is to prevent nonmembers from receiving free benefits of the union in contract negotiations. The problem, then, is how to determine whether an employee who pays only these required fees is a member of the union.

In general, an employee who only pays his required initiation fee and dues is not considered a full member. In order to retain the status of nonmember in a situation where he is paying dues, a person must carefully refrain from any act which exceeds the minimum legal obligation. If he does exceed the minimum by taking the union oath, for instance, he may be deemed to have indicated an intention to become a full member. Since it has been held that a union may require only these minimum payments from an employee,[98] then the union may not require him to do anything else, including to follow its rules. Under

---

[97] Radio Officers Union v. NLRB, 347 U.S. 17, 33 L.R.R.M. 2417 (1954).

[98] *Id.* at 41, 33 L.R.R.M. at 2426.

a contract theory, a requirement to follow union rules would clearly be unenforceable since a "contract" was not entered into voluntarily.[99] The General Counsel and Assistant General Counsel of the UAW, the union involved in both *Allis-Chalmers* and *Scofield,* have written an article in which they stated:

> Obviously, an employee who tenders dues to a union merely to satisfy a contractual requirement, as in *Union Starch & Refining Co.* v. *NLRB,* does not enjoy all of the provisions of full union membership, nor does he submit to union rules, regulations, or discipline.[100]

Having met his legal obligation, he should not suddenly find himself subject to union discipline.

At the other end of the spectrum is the employee who has met his financial obligations, taken a membership oath, participated in union activities, received union benefits, and represented himself as a union member. Such an employee obviously should be considered a member and subject therefore to legitimate union discipline.

In between these two extremes, exists a wide variety of positions which an employee may occupy. The action necessary to alter an employee's status from nonmember to member is unclear. The Supreme Court has offered little guidance. In *Allis-Chalmers,* where the Court found the employees full members, it noted that: employees had taken the oath of full membership; two employees had participated in meetings where strike votes were taken, and no proof was offered to contradict this evidence of membership.[101] The Court, however, neither specified which of these elements supported a finding for full membership, nor clarified whether the union or the employee had the burden of proving full membership. Therefore, if an employee participates in union activities or receives union benefits, he risks being considered a union member.

The problem of distinguishing a union member from a nonmember raises the question: how meaningful is the member-nonmember distinction to the average worker? Does he realize that he has a choice? Does he realize the rights that he relinquishes when he becomes a member? Is his choice an in-

---

[99] 388 U.S. at 208, 65 L.R.R.M. at 2462.

[100] Schlossberg & Lubin, *supra* note 52, at 210.

[101] 388 U.S. at 196, 65 L.R.R.M. at 2457.

formed and reasoned one, or is it uninformed and the product of peer pressure? Since the cost of being a member is the same (or sometimes less than)[102] the cost of being a nonmember,[103] and since members can receive certain benefits such as pension and death benefits, an employee may become a member for membership advantages without ever knowing its disadvantages or even the possibility of free choice.

One commentator has suggested that the union assume the burden of full disclosure to the employee before he makes his decision.

> In an era when the courts and the legislatures are increasingly aware of the fact that the consumer buying corn flakes in the grocery store can not adequately protect himself against deceptive practices, and that the borrower trying to finance his automobile can not bargain independently with the lender, and that the investor must have an agency and a detailed set of regulations to insure his protection against financiers, it is scarcely radical to suggest that a working man has the right to insist that his union assume the burden of full disclosure before he waives important statutory and constitutional rights and exposes himself to penalties in the thousands of dollars.[104]

Such disclosure would at least demonstrate that the employee has an opportunity for a reasoned choice by knowing his options and their advantages and disadvantages. It would also put the burden of proof concerning membership where it should be—on the party trying to curtail the freedom of the individual.

Since the avowed purpose of a union security clause is to prevent freeloaders from obtaining the benefits of a collective bargaining agreement without having to share the costs, nonmembers who are required to pay dues should not have to pay more than their fair share of the bargaining costs. They should not be forced to contribute to such programs as the

---

102 Local 171, Pulp and Paper Workers (Boise Cascade Corp.), 165 N.L.R.B. 971, 65 L.R.R.M. 1382 (1967). The Board allowed the union to refund $2 of the members' monthly dues to those who attended the union's meetings.

103 The cost of paying dues may be reduced, to some extent, if the employee is able to itemize his deductions on his federal income tax return. The Internal Revenue Service has ruled that union dues are deductible by a member, and, if their payment is a condition of employment, by a nonmember. They are deductible, however, only if the employee itemizes his deductions. Treas. Reg. § 1.162-15(c) (1975); Rev. Rul. 54-190, 1954-1 CUM. BULL. 46; Rev. Rul. 68-82, 1968-1 CUM. BULL. 68.

104 Seham, *Limitations Upon and Directions of a Union's Right to Discipline Its Members*, N.Y.U. 25th CONF. OF LAB. 191, 199 (1972).

union pension fund. The employee should be given a clear choice by the union, reasonably explained, so that he knows his alternatives. If he chooses not to join, his dues should be only for his share of the total bargaining costs.

One of Justice Black's criticisms of the majority decision in *Allis-Chalmers* is that employees may not know they have a choice, may not know how properly to express their choice, and may be afraid to exercise their Section 7 rights for fear that they will be unable to convince the Board or the courts of their true status.[105] By requiring the union to explain their choices, employees will be able to avoid these problems.

Resignation

Prior to the *Allis-Chalmers* case, almost no unions had in their bylaws provisions relating to resignation. It was commonly understood that one simply ceased paying dues in order to resign from union membership. Since *Allis-Chalmers*, a few unions have amended their by-laws with regard to resignation procedures.

The Supreme Court has considered two cases dealing with an employee's right to resign from a union and subsequently disregard union rules. The first case was *NLRB v. Granite State Joint Board, Textile Workers, Local 1029.*[106] In this case, the Court had to determine when a union's power to regulate the conduct of its members ends. May a union member resign at any time and thereafter be free of union discipline for subsequent acts, or may a union restrict a member's right to resign during a strike where solidarity is needed?

Granite State

Justice Douglas summarized the facts for the Court:

> Respondent is a union that had a collective-bargaining agreement with an employer which contained a maintenance-of-membership clause providing that members were, as a condition of employment, to remain in good standing "as to payment of dues" for the duration of the contract. Neither the contract nor the Union's constitution or bylaws contained any provision defining or limiting the circumstances under which a member could resign. A few days before the collective agreement expired, the Union membership voted to strike if no agreement was reached by a given date. No agreement

---

[105] 388 U.S. at 215, 65 L.R.R.M. at 2465.

[106] 409 U.S. 213, 81 L.R.R.M. 2853 (1972).

was reached in the specified period, so the strike and attendant picketing commenced. Shortly thereafter, the Union held a meeting at which the membership resolved that any member aiding or abetting the employer during the strike would be subject to a $2,000 fine.

About six weeks later, two members sent the Union their letters of resignation. Six months or more later, 29 other members resigned. These 31 employees returned to work.

The union gave them notice that charges had been made against them and that on given dates the Union would hold trials. None of the 31 employees appeared on the dates prescribed; but the trials nonetheless took place even in the absence of the employees and fines [equivalent to a day's wages for each day worked during the strike] were imposed on all. Suits were filed by the Union to collect the fines. But the outcome was not determined because the employees filed unfair labor practice charges with the National Labor Relations Board against the Union.[107]

The Board found the union guilty of violating Section 8(b) (1)(A) of the Act,[108] but the First Circuit Court of Appeals refused to enforce the Board's order.[109]

Justice Douglas, joined by seven other justices, reversed the court of appeals and affirmed the Board's decision. Justice Burger filed a concurring opinion, and Justice Blackmun was the only dissenter. The Court held:

> Where a member lawfully resigns from a union and thereafter engages in conduct which the union rule proscribes the union commits an unfair labor practice when it seeks enforcement of fines for that conduct.[110]

The Court distinguished this from *Allis-Chalmers*. In that case, the fines were permitted levied against those who "enjoyed full union membership." [111] This was not the case in *Granite State* since the employees had resigned from the union. "[W]hen a member lawfully resigns from the union, its power over him ends." [112]

---

[107] *Id.* at 214, 81 L.R.R.M. at 2853-54.

[108] Textile Workers, Local 1029 (International Paper Box Machine Co.), 187 N.L.R.B. No. 90, 70 L.R.R.M. 1246 (1970).

[109] NLRB v. Granite State Joint Board, Textile Workers, Local 1029, 446 F.2d 369, 77 L.R.R.M. 2711 (1st Cir. 1971).

[110] 409 U.S. at 217, 81 L.R.R.M. at 2854.

[111] *Id.* at 215, 81 L.R.R.M. at 2854.

[112] *Id.*, 81 L.R.R.M. at 2854.

The Court held that when the right to resign is not restricted by the union's constitution or bylaws,

> [W]e have . . . only to apply the law which normally is reflected in our free institutions—the right of the individual to join or to resign from associations, as he sees fit. . . .[113]

The Court refused to indicate the extent to which a union constitution or bylaws may curtail the freedom to resign.[114] Justice Burger, in his concurring opinion, suggested that he might not allow any limitations on a member's right to resign.[115]

The one dissenting opinion indicated that once the members approved the strike, the strikebreaking penalties, and participated in the strike, they had voluntarily undertaken a course of action that they were not free to abandon.

> The mutual reliance of his fellow members who abide by the strike for which they have all voted outweighs, in the circumstances here presented, the admitted interests of the individual who resigns to return to work. He may still resign, and he may also return to work, but not without the prospect of having to pay a reasonable union fine for which he voted.[116]

The majority opinion in this case is persuasive. It is, as the Court pointed out, consistent with the normal rules governing membership in voluntary organizations. It is also consistent with the Court's contract theory used in *Allis-Chalmers*. When the contract terms do not limit the right to terminate the contractual relationship, the parties can do so at will. In addition, this decision reinforces the Court's statement in *Scofield* that for a rule to be enforceable, it must be imposed upon union members who are free to leave the union and escape the rule.

---

[113] *Id.* at 216, 81 L.R.R.M. at 2854.

[114] *Id.* at 217, 81 L.R.R.M. at 2855.

[115] ". . . the institutional needs of the Union, important though they are, do not outweigh the rights and needs of the individual. . . . Where the individual employee has freely chosen to exercise his legal right to abandon the privileges of union membership, it is not for us to impose the obligation of continued membership." *Id.* at 218, 81 L.R.R.M. at 2855.

[116] *Id.* at 223, 81 L.R.R.M. at 2857.

Booster Lodge

In 1973, the Court faced a similar case, *Booster Lodge 405, IAM v. NLRB.*[117] The union attempted to distinguish this case from *Granite State* on the grounds that in this case, the union constitution had a provision expressly prohibiting members from strikebreaking. The union argued that this agreement not to strikebreak would still be binding on a member who resigned during a strike. The Court, in a per curiam opinion, rejected this argument. Again, as in *Granite State,* the Court found that the agreement between the union and the member terminated upon his resignation.[118] It again specifically left open the question of a union's right to restrict the member's right to resign.[119]

In this case, Justice Blackmun, the lone dissenter in *Granite State,* concurred with the rest of the Court. He distinguished the cases because in *Booster Lodge* the member did not have any notice that he was waiving his Section 7 rights. The penalty was not approved by the membership, and the members were not informed of any penalty for post-resignation strikebreaking.

Under the Court's decisions in *Granite State* and *Booster Lodge,* a union member is free to resign from his union and escape discipline for his subsequent acts if the union constitution or bylaws do not limit this right. This raises the dual questions of what constitutes effective resignation and whether a union may, by a provision in its constitution or bylaws, limit a member's right to resign.

When Is a Resignation Effective?

The Board has said that where a union's constitution is silent, ". . . a member is free to resign at will by clearly conveying to the union his unequivocal intent to resign."[120] Apparently, no specific steps are required; a member must clearly inform the union of his intention to resign.[121]

---

[117] 412 U.S. 84, 83 L.R.R.M. 2189 (1973).

[118] *Id.* at 89-90, 83 L.R.R.M. at 2192.

[119] *Id.* at 88, 83 L.R.R.M. at 2191.

[120] District Lodge 99, IAM (General Electric Co.), 194 N.L.R.B. No. 163, 938, 79 L.R.R.M. 1208 (1972).

[121] Communications Workers, Local 6135 (Southwestern Bell Telephone Co.), 188 N.L.R.B., No. 144, 76 L.R.R.M. 1635 (1971).

For example, the Board has held, and the First Circuit has agreed, that when a union member, in a discussion with his union's president, said he was resigning, crumpled and threw away his union card, and said "I quit," he had effectively resigned.[122] Likewise, the Board has held that a member who revoked his dues check-off authorization and returned his membership card to the union gave clear and effective notice of his resignation.[123]

On the other hand, a California court has held that a member does not effectively resign by telling a union officer that he does so in a chance, casual meeting.[124] Apparently, to that court, the atmosphere of such a chance meeting is not sufficiently serious to convey effectively a desire to resign.

Along similar lines, a member's conversation with his local's financial secretary stating that he is *thinking* of resigning and wants to stop having dues taken from his paycheck, plus a letter to the company canceling his dues check-off authorization, is not sufficient notice of resignation.[125] He has not clearly indicated that he wants to resign. A member can think about quitting, and a member may cancel his dues check off and plan to pay his dues directly. Also, a member does not have to submit his resignation himself. The Board has held that a member may have his attorney submit the resignation.[126]

A member's resignation is effective when it is received by the union. Thus, a fine for crossing a picket line on the day the letter of resignation was received has been upheld since the evidence did not show whether the resignation or the strikebreaking occurred first.[127]

[122] Mechanical & Allied Production Workers, Local 444 (Pneumatic Scale Corp.), 173 N.L.R.B. 325, 69 L.R.R.M. 1384 (1968), *enforced*, 427 F.2d 883, 74 L.R.R.M. 2457 (1st Cir. 1970).

[123] Communications Workers, Local 6135 (Southwestern Bell Telephone Co.), 188 N.L.R.B. No. 144, 76 L.R.R.M. 1635 (1971).

[124] District Council v. Smith, 61 L.R.R.M. 2208 (Santa Barbara, Calif. Mun. Ct. 1966).

[125] District Lodge 99, IAM (General Electric Co.), 194 N.L.R.B. No. 163, 79 L.R.R.M. 1208 (1972).

[126] United Construction Workers, Local 10 (Erhardt Construction Co.), 187 N.L.R.B. No. 99, 76 L.R.R.M. 1121 (1971).

[127] *Id.*, 76 L.R.R.M. 1121.

May a Union Restrict the Right to Resign?

The last question in the area of membership and resignation is whether a union may restrict a member's right to resign by a provision in its constitution or bylaws. Many union constitutions do place some restrictions on a member's right to resign.[128] Such restrictions obviously impinge on the individual's rights. The union's interest, however, in these restrictions is unclear. Captive membership, per se, does not seem to be a legitimate union interest. Solidarity during bargaining and strikes, however, may be a legitimate rationale for such a rule. The need for financial stability may justify some restrictions, but this is questionable.

The UAW, in its constitution, requires that resignations be submitted to the local's financial secretary within ten days prior to the end of the year.[129] In 1962, the Board held that this provision did not effectively limit the right of a member to

---

[128] *E.g.*, the *Constitution of the International Ladies' Garment Workers' Union*, Art. 16, § 1 (1971) provides:

Article 16
WITHDRAWAL FROM MEMBERSHIP

Section 1.　Requirements for withdrawal card

(a) A member who wishes to leave the industry may withdraw from membership in the I.L.G.W.U. and be given an official withdrawal card if he gives written notice of such withdrawal, pays all fixed dues, assessments, fines and other charges against him to the date of his withdrawal and surrenders his membership book or card.

(b) A member who has so withdrawn and who has subsequently been readmitted shall not thereafter be eligible for withdrawal until six months after his readmission.

The *Constitution of the International Brotherhood of Teamsters, Chauffers, Warehousemen and Helpers of America*, Art. II, § (3) (1971) provides:

(h) No member may resign from his membership in the International Union or any subordinate body before he has paid all dues, assessments, fines and other obligations owing to the International Union and all its subordinate bodies, and no resignation shall become effective until such payment.

[129] *Constitution of the International Union, U.A.W.*, Art. 6, §§ 17-18 (1972) :

A member may resign or terminate his membership only if he is in good standing, is not in arrears or delinquent in the payment of any dues or other financial obligations to the International Union or to his Local Union and there are no charges filed and pending against him. Such resignation or termination shall be effective only if by written communication, signed by the member, and sent by registered or certified mail, return receipt requested, to the Financial Secretary of the Local Union within the ten (10) day period prior to the end of the fiscal year of the Local Union as fixed by this Constitution. . . .

resign at will.[130] The First Circuit Court of Appeals disagreed and refused to enforce the Board's order.[131] It found that the union's restriction on resignation was reasonable since it was aimed at preserving the union's financial stability. Therefore, the resignations submitted without complying with the constitution were not effective.

This approach has been criticized on several grounds. It severely limits the right to resign and may not give the employee the option to do so at any relevant time. He may be unable to resign at or after the time a policy is decided, when a strike is called, or during a strike. At all of the critical times, the employee may be locked into the union.[132] In addition, financial stability is a poor excuse for limiting so drastically the right to resign. Although membership guaranteed for some period may be desirable to promote short-term stability, eleven and two-thirds months is far too long. If financial stability were a valid goal, a member should be able to resign at will but be required to continue paying dues for a while. The Board again recently held this provision ineffective, this time relying on *Scofield*.

In its 1972 decision holding invalid the constitutional provision restricting union resignation to ten days prior to the end of the year,[133] the Board held:

> . . . the provision imposes such narrow restrictions as to amount, in effect, to a denial to members of a voluntary method of severing their relationship with the Union. In short, the present provision does not make it possible for a member to avail himself of the "strategy" of leaving the Union as recognized by the Board in *Boeing* and envisioned by Supreme Court in *Scofield* . . . .
>
> We cannot view union members as being "free to leave the union" when their right to leave is as narrowly restricted as it is here.[134]

---

[130] UAW, Local 899 (John L. Paulding, Inc.), 137 N.L.R.B. 901, 50 L.R.R.M. 1283 (1962).

[131] NLRB v. UAW, 320 F.2d 12, 53 L.R.R.M. 2768 (1st Cir. 1963).

[132] Gould, *Some Limitations Upon Union Discipline Under the National Labor Relations Act: The Radiations of Allis-Chalmers,* 1970 DUKE L. REV. 1067, 1105 (1970).

[133] UAW (General Electric Co.), 197 N.L.R.B. No. 93, 80 L.R.R.M. 1411 (1972).

[134] *Id.* at 609, 80 L.R.R.M. at 1412.

In two subsequent cases, the Board has adhered to, and re-affirmed, this position.[135] The Board's approach here seems far more persuasive than that of the First Circuit.[136]

In order to restrict the right of a member to resign, the union rule must serve a legitimate union interest. Since it impinges on individual rights so obviously, it must be narrowly written if it is to be valid. Neither the Board nor the Supreme Court has ruled on whether any restrictions are valid. Since the Court's decisions in *Granite State* and *Booster Lodge* have held that a union may not limit the right to resign unless it does so in its constitution or bylaws, it seems likely that some unions will alter their bylaws accordingly. Litigation on this issue seems likely in the not too distant future.

REASONABLENESS OF FINES

Both in *Allis-Chalmers* and in *Scofield*, the Supreme Court pointed out that the fines imposed were reasonable in amount. The Court did not address the issue of whether the size of a fine could constitute a violation of Section 8(b)(1)(A). This issue was brought before the Court in *NLRB v. Boeing Co.*[137] Can a fine be so unreasonably large as to be coercive or may a union impose whatever size fine the "contract" allows?

Boeing

Boeing is a companion case to *Booster Lodge*. The union fined strikebreaking members $450 each, and the company filed an unfair labor practice charge based on the size of the fines. The Board found that the fines did not violate the Act,[138] but the D.C. Circuit Court reversed and remanded the case to the Board.[139] The case was then appealed to the Supreme Court.

---

[135] UAW, Local 469 (Master Lock Co.), 221 N.L.R.B. No. 125, 90 L.R.R.M. 1563 (1975); Local 1384, UAW (Ex-Cell-O Corp.), 219 N.L.R.B. No. 123 (1975).

[136] The Board did not decide whether any provision in the union's constitution could legitimately limit a member's right to resign. *Id.*, 80 L.R.R.M. at 1412.

[137] 412 U.S. 67, 83 L.R.R.M. 2183 (1973).

[138] Booster Lodge No. 405, IAM (Boeing Co.), 185 N.L.R.B. 380, 383 n. 16, 75 L.R.R.M. 1004, 1007 n. 16 (1970).

[139] Booster Lodge No. 405, IAM v. NLRB, 459 F.2d 1143, 79 L.R.R.M. 2443 (D.C. Cir. 1972).

Justice Rehnquist, joined by five other justices, delivered the majority opinion. The Court held that the Board should not examine the reasonableness of the fines. Such questions should be settled in state courts.

The Court first noted that whatever it said in *Allis-Chalmers* and *Scofield* concerning a requirement of reasonableness was simply dictum. To the extent that it said fines must be reasonable, the Court rejected that dictum.[140]

The Court found that the amount of a fine which is otherwise enforceable is a matter of contract between the member and the union. As such,

> [i]ssues as to the reasonableness or unreasonableness of such fines must be decided upon the basis of the law of contracts, voluntary associations, or such other principles of law as may be applied in a forum competent to adjudicate the issue. Under our holding, state courts will be wholly free to apply state law to such issues at the suit of either the union or the member fined.[141]

The Court rejected the arguments of the circuit court and the dissenters for having the Board determine reasonableness. It concluded that the Board's expertise is not required and that a need for consistent decisions does not dictate a contrary result.

The Court noted that it did not believe its opinion would result in any undue hardships for members. It pointed out, as it had in *Allis-Chalmers*, that,

> . . . state courts, in reviewing the imposition of union discipline, find ways to strike down "discipline [which] involves a severe hardship." [142]

The Court went on to state that in reviewing state court cases both before and after *Allis-Chalmers* and *Scofield,* it found that state courts "are quite willing to determine whether disciplinary fines are reasonable in amount." [143] The Court then gave examples, in a footnote, of state cases holding fines reasonable or unreasonable.[144]

Three justices dissented. Justice Douglas, joined by Chief Justice Burger and Justice Blackmun, found the need for Board

---

[140] 412 U.S. at 72, 83 L.R.R.M. at 2185.

[141] *Id.* at 74, 83 L.R.R.M. at 2186.

[142] *Id.* at 76, 83 L.R.R.M. at 2186.

[143] *Id.*

[144] *Id.* n. 12, 83 L.R.R.M. at 2186 n. 12.

expertise in this area. Moreover, Douglas feared that the cost and trouble of litigating the issue in state courts might prevent unreasonable fines from being contested.

Since the Court views the relationship between a union and its members as contractual, and since it has held that fines are not coercive, the majority decision seems the more persuasive in this case. The fine itself is obviously acceptable under the Court's decision in *Allis-Chalmers*. The relationship between the union and the member, as defined by the union's constitution, should determine the size of the fine. This is a matter for the states since it is a matter of equity in which state courts have more concern than the Board.

UNION DISCIPLINE OF SUPERVISORS

A supervisor may also be a member of a union. In recent years, there has been considerable litigation dealing with the disciplinary power that unions have over these members. One area of controversy concerns whether Section 8(b)(1)(B)[145] of the Act protects a supervisor-member who is also the employer or the owner of the employing business. The second area of controversy concerns whether Section 8(b)(1)(B) protects supervisor-members from all union discipline or only from discipline for certain offenses. The Supreme Court recently addressed itself to the latter issue in *Florida Power & Light Co. v. IBEW, Local 641.*[146]

Supervisor-Member-Owners

In some situations, the owner of a business may also be a union member. If, for a valid reason, a union decides to discipline such a member-owner for his actions as management's collective bargainer or grievance adjustor, may it do so, or is such a supervisor-member-owner protected by Section 8(b)(1)(B)? The Board has held that Section 8(b)(1)(B) does not protect a supervisor-member from sanctions against him by his

---

[145] NLRA § 8(b)(1)(B), 29 U.S.C. § 158(b)(1)(B) (1970).

It shall be an unfair labor practice for a labor organization or its agents (1) to restrain or coerce . . . (B) an employer in the selection of his representatives for the purposes of collective bargaining or the adjustment of grievances.

[146] 417 U.S. 790, 86 L.R.R.M. 2689 (1974).

union when he is also the sole owner of the employer.[147] The Board has explained its conclusion this way:

> The legislative history behind Section 8(b)(1)(B) makes it clear that Congress was only concerned with protecting employers in the selection of their representatives for the two purposes provided therein; there is no indication that Congress intended to protect the employer himself against such fines and sanctions. There is no restraint or coercion against the employer *in the selection of his representatives* for the prohibited objects where the employer himself is acting as the representative for these purposes. This dichotomy in treatment of union sanctions imposed on an employer's supervisors as opposed to those levied directly against the employer himself may also be explained by the fact that it is difficult to envision circumstances where the employer would be greatly influenced in the performance of his grievance-adjustment or collective-bargaining functions where any decision he makes in those respects directly works to his benefit or detriment depending on how he decides it.[148]
>
> [Emphasis by the Board; footnotes omitted.]

In addition to the situation where the supervisor-member is the sole owner, the Board has also extended this rationale to cases where the supervisor-member has a majority,[149] or even a minority interest.[150] The Board has held that a union is ". . . free to fine those supervisor-member-owners whose ownership interest is so substantial so as to make them the employer."[151] In that case, the Board held that a supervisor-member-owner is an employer if he either personally, or together with other family members, has more than a 25 percent ownership interest in the company.[152] It is not yet clear whether this 25 percent test will become a hard and fast rule or will vary with the circumstances.

---

[147] Bricklayers, Masons and Plasterers' Union, Local No. 1 (Barr Floors, Inc.), 209 N.L.R.B. 820, 85 L.R.R.M. 1553 (1974); Local 146, Sheet Metal Workers (Robert Dales Jones d/b/a Aarctic Heating and Cooling Company), 203 N.L.R.B. 1090, 83 L.R.R.M. 1253 (1973).

[148] Painters, Local 1621 (Glass Management Ass'n), 221 N.L.R.B. No. 91, 90 L.R.R.M. 1637, 1640 (1975).

[149] International Association of Heat and Frost Insulators and Asbestos Workers, Local 19 (Insulation Industries, Inc.), 211 N.L.R.B. No. 86, 86 L.R.R.M. 1427 (1974).

[150] Painters, Local 1621 (Glass Management Ass'n), 221 N.L.R.B. No. 91, 90 L.R.R.M. 1637 (1975).

[151] *Id.,* 90 L.R.R.M. at 1641.

[152] *Id.,* 90 L.R.R.M. at 1641.

Thus, the Board has read Section 8(b)(1)(B) as not protecting supervisor-member-owners from union disciplinary action. The Board and the courts have also had to determine what protection Section 8(b)(1)(B) does afford supervisor-members. This issue reached the Supreme Court in *Florida Power & Light Co.*

Florida Power & Light Co.

In this case, the Court had to decide whether a union may fine supervisory members who cross picket lines and perform rank and file work during a strike. Is the supervisor performing a legitimate supervisory function and therefore immune from discipline under Section 8(b)(1)(B), or is the supervisor not protected by Section 8(b)(1)(B) and therefore subject to legitimate union discipline as is any other union member?

The Court considered two cases that were consolidated for argument by the D.C. Circuit Court. In one case, the union fined supervisory members for crossing the union's picket line and performing rank and file work. A group of supervisors, acting as the Bell Telephone Protective Association, filed charges with the Board alleging that the union had violated Section 8(b)(1)(B). The Board found an unfair labor practice,[153] and a panel of the D.C. Circuit affirmed the decision.[154] In the other case, the union also fined supervisory members for crossing picket lines and performing rank and file work. The company filed charges with the Board alleging a Section 8(b)(1)(B) violation. The Board again held that the union had committed an unfair labor practice.[155] The D.C. Circuit then decided to consolidate the two cases and hear them en banc. In a five to four decision, the D.C. Circuit Court reversed the decision of its panel and refused to enforce the Board's orders.[156]

The Supreme Court, also in a five to four decision, affirmed the D.C. Circuit Court's decision. Justice Stewart delivered the opinion of the Court, and Justice White filed the dissenting

---

[153] IBEW, Local 134 (Illinois Bell Telephone Co.), 192 N.L.R.B. No. 17, 77 L.R.R.M. 1610 (1971).

[154] IBEW v. NLRB, 487 F.2d 1113, 81 L.R.R.M. 2257 (D.C. Cir. 1972).

[155] IBEW, System Council U-4 (Florida Power & Light Co.), 193 N.L.R.B. No. 7, 78 L.R.R.M. 1065 (1971).

[156] IBEW v. NLRB, 487 F.2d 1143, 83 L.R.R.M. 2583 (D.C. Cir. 1973).

opinion in which Chief Justice Burger and Justices Blackmun and Rehnquist joined.

Justice Stewart read Section 8(b) (1) (B) to,

> . . . reflect a clearly focused congressional concern with the protection of employers in the selection of representatives to engage in two particular and explicitly stated activities, namely collective bargaining and the adjustment of grievances.[157]

He found that the legislative history supports a narrow reading of the section.

> Nowhere in the legislative history is there to be found any implication that Congress sought to extend protection to the employer from union restraint or coercion when engaged in any activity other than the *selection* of its representatives for the purpose of collective bargaining and grievance adjustment. The conclusion is thus inescapable that a union's discipline of one of its members who is a supervisory employee can constitute a violation of § 8(b)(1)(B) only when that discipline may adversely affect the supervisor's conduct in performing the duties of, and acting in his capacity as, grievance adjuster or collective bargainer on behalf of the employer.[158]

Since the supervisors who were fined were not engaged in collective bargaining or in adjusting grievances, he concluded that they were not protected by Section 8(b) (1) (B).

The majority agreed that allowing such fines might deprive an employer of the full allegiance of his supervisors in the future. It found, however, that the solution, should the employer be concerned, is to refuse to hire union members as supervisors.

The minority argued that the Board's broader reading of Section 8(b) (1) (B) was "a fair and reasonable interpretation." [159] It concluded:

> This Court is not a Super-Board authorized to overrule an agency's choice between reasonable constructions of the controlling statute. We should not impose our views on the Board as long as it stays within the outer boundaries of the statute it is charged with administering.[160]

---

[157] 417 U.S. at 803, 86 L.R.R.M. at 2693-94.

[158] *Id.* at 804-5, 86 L.R.R.M. at 2694.

[159] *Id.* at 813, 86 L.R.R.M. at 2697.

[160] *Id.* at 816, 86 L.R.R.M. at 2698.

The majority's opinion is the more persuasive. As the majority pointed out, Section 8(b) (1) (B) was apparently designed to protect the employer from coercion in this narrow area. If Congress meant to protect the employer's supervisors from all coercion it could have done so. It chose instead to limit the protection from restraint or coercion in selecting representatives for two specific supervisory functions.

The Court's decision is likely to have at least one undesirable result. Management, in order to ensure the undivided loyalty of its supervisors, may stop using union members as supervisors. This, in turn, may make it more difficult for management to obtain well qualified supervisors, and it may make it more difficult for an employee to work his way up into management. A union member with seniority and union benefits such as pension, old age, and death benefits, may be reluctant to resign from the union and lose his job security and union benefits. If this happens, management will have to look elsewhere for supervisors.

How narrowly or broadly the functions of adjusting grievances and bargaining collectively should be interpreted is not clear from the Court's decision. The Court referred to, but did not rule on the validity of, the Board's decision in *San Francisco-Oakland Mailers' Union No. 18 (Northwest Publications, Inc.)*.[161] There, the Board found that the union violated Section 8(b) (1) (B) by disciplining supervisory members "for allegedly assigning bargaining unit work in violation of the collective-bargaining agreement."[162] The Board and circuit courts have, on a number of occasions,

> . . . extended § 8(b) (1)(B) to proscribe union discipline of management representatives both for the manner in which they performed their collective-bargaining and grievance-adjusting functions, and for the manner in which they performed other supervisory functions if those representatives also in fact possessed authority to bargain collectively or to adjust grievances.[163]

In several cases decided after the Court's decision in *Florida Power & Light Co.*, the Board has had to face this issue.

In *Florida Power & Light Co.*, the supervisor-members were disciplined only for doing rank and file work. Those supervisor-

---

[161] 172 N.L.R.B. No. 252, 69 L.R.R.M. 1157 (1968).

[162] 417 U.S. at 800, 86 L.R.R.M. 2692.

[163] *Id.*, 86 L.R.R.M. at 2692-93.

members who crossed the picket lines only to perform their normal supervisory functions were not disciplined. Relying on this fact, and citing Justice White's comment in his dissent which stated:

> I do not read the Court to say that § 8(b)(1)(B) would allow a union to discipline supervisor-members for performing supervisory or management functions, as opposed to customary rank-and-file work, during a labor dispute[,][164]

the Board has held that it is a violation of Section 8(b)(1)(B) for a union to discipline a supervisor-member for engaging in any supervisory activity—not just grievance adjusting or collective bargaining.[165] This is because the Board views any such discipline as likely to affect adversely the supervisor's conduct in performing the duties of, and acting in his capacity as, grievance adjuster or collective bargainer.[166] Going a step farther, the Board held that this rationale applies, and discipline is forbidden, even if the supervisor-member did perform a *minimal* amount of rank and file work.[167] When, however, more than a minimal amount of rank and file work is performed, the union is allowed to discipline the supervisor-member.[168]

The Board has stated that its determination of whether union discipline of a supervisor-member violates Section 8(b)(1)(B) hinges,

> . . . on the comparative amount of bargaining unit work, as opposed to normal supervisory functions, which the [supervisor-member] performed while working behind the picket line.[169]

---

[164] *Id.* at 815, 86 L.R.R.M. at 6298.

[165] Writers Guild of Am. (West, Inc.), 217 N.L.R.B. No. 159, 89 L.R.R.M. 1221 (1975); Chicago Typographical Union No. 16 (Hammond Publishers, Inc.), 216 N.L.R.B. No. 149, 88 L.R.R.M. 1378 (1975); New York Typographical Union No. 6 (Daily Racing Form, a subsidiary of Triangle Publications, Inc.), 216 N.L.R.B. No. 147, 88 L.R.R.M. 1384 (1975).

[166] *See* cases cited in note 165.

[167] Painters, Local 1621 (Glass Management Ass'n), 221 N.L.R.B. No. 91, 90 L.R.R.M. 1637 (1975); Chicago Typograhpical Union No. 16 (Hammond Publishers, Inc.), 216 N.L.R.B. No. 149, 88 L.R.R.M. 1378 (1975).

[168] Painters, Local 1621 (Glass Management Ass'n), 221 N.L.R.B. No. 91, 90 L.R.R.M. 1637 (1975); Carpenters, Local No. 14 (Max M. Kaplan Properties), 217 N.L.R.B. No. 13, 89 L.R.R.M. 1002 (1975); Bakery and Confectionery Workers, Locals 24 and 119 (Food Employees Council, Inc.), 216 N.L.R.B. No. 150, 88 L.R.R.M. 1390 (1975).

[169] Painters, Local 1621 (Glass Management Ass'n), 221 N.L.R.B. No. 91, 90 L.R.R.M. 1637, 1639 (1975).

These decisions limit the scope of the Supreme Court's holding in *Florida Power and Light Company*. If the Board is correct in its interpretation, then the adverse impact of that decision is less than was originally feared. As long as the supervisor-member is performing any supervisory function, the employer is entitled to the supervisor's undivided loyalty. It is only when he is engaged in more than minimal rank and file work that the supervisor-member owes loyalty to his union, too.

In sum, for discipline to be proper, it must be for violation of a rule that the union has a legitimate interest in enforcing. Generally, such a rule promotes the union's ability to serve as the exclusive bargaining agent of those it represents. The rule must not be contrary to public policy. The Board and the courts have found that a union may not discipline a member for utilizing the Board or the courts, or for performing his civic duties; a union may not require a member to violate the law or a contract, nor limit his speech and assembly rights. A union may take direct disciplinary action only against its members. Generally, an employee will be considered a union member if he receives union benefits or participates in union activities.

The Supreme Court's decisions in *Granite State* and *Booster Lodge* have held that a union may not limit the right to resign unless it does so in its constitution or bylaws. The rule must be narrowly written if it is to be valid, but neither the Board nor the Court has ruled on whether any restrictions are valid. In addition, the Board has interpreted the Court's decision in *Florida Power & Light Co.* to hold that it is a violation of Section 8(b)(1)(B) for a union to discipline a supervisor-member for engaging in any supervisory activity, and also to forbid discipline even if the supervisor-member did perform a *minimal* amount of rank and file work.

The Federal Procedural Law

In the late 1950s, Congressional attention began to focus increasingly on corruption within labor organizations. To a large extent, this was a result of the investigations and revelations of the Select Committee on Improper Activities in the Labor or Management Field (The McClellan Committee).[1] In 1958, Congress began formulating legislation to end some of the abuses it perceived within labor organizations. After various proposals, unsuccessful bills, amendments, and compromises, the Labor-Management Reporting and Disclosure Act of 1959 (Landrum-Griffin Act) was enacted and became law on September 14, 1959.[2]

Title I of the Act, the "Bill of Rights of Members of Labor Organizations," was added as an amendment to protect various fundamental rights of the individual union members.[3] It guarantees all members a variety of rights including safeguards against improper disciplinary action.

Section 101(a)(5) of the Act states the procedural rules which unions must follow when disciplining members:

> No member of any labor organization may be fined, suspended, expelled, or otherwise disciplined except for nonpayment of dues by such an organization or by any officer thereof unless such member has been (a) served with written specific charges; (b) given a reasonable time to prepare his defense; (c) afforded a full and fair hearing.[4]

Enforcement of these procedural safeguards is provided for in the Act by Section 102 which states:

---

[1] Rothman, *Legislative History of the "Bill of Rights" for Union Members*, 45 MINN. L. REV. 199, 204 (1960).

[2] 73 Stat. 519 (1959), *as amended*, 29 U.S.C. §§ 401-531 (1970).

[3] Rothman, *supra* note 1, at 206-7.

[4] 29 U.S.C. § 411(a)(5) (1970).

Any person whose rights secured by the provisions of this title have been infringed by any violation of this title may bring a civil action in a district court of the United States for such relief (including injunctions) as may be appropriate. . . .[5]

The Act provides that the rules it sets forth are minimum requirements, not meant to limit the rights and remedies of union members.[6] Therefore, the states are permitted to impose a stricter set of procedural requirements on labor unions. Likewise, the unions themselves may adopt stricter requirements.

This chapter examines the decisions of the federal courts to ascertain how these provisions of the Act have been interpreted. It will attempt to delineate the procedural rules regulating union discipline of members.

WHAT CONSTITUTES DISCIPLINE?

Section 101(a)(5) is designed to protect union members from improper disciplinary action by their union. It defines certain kinds of discipline—fines, suspension, and expulsion—as subjects of regulation. It also regulates other sanctions under the phrase "otherwise disciplined." This phrase, however, is not defined by the Act. The federal courts, therefore, have been responsible for interpreting it. In some areas, there is substantial agreement concerning the disciplinary nature of an action. In other areas, however, the courts are in conflict.

The Act requires that the discipline be administered by a labor "organization or any officer thereof." This means that discipline must flow from the organization itself or from a union officer acting in his official capacity. Thus, actions of individual members or union officials not acting in their official capacity do not give rise to an action under Section 101(a)(5).[7]

The second requirement for discipline is that the union member must suffer some detriment. Thus, where a member was merely reprimanded by the chair at a meeting, no discipline, within the meaning of the Act, occurred.[8] Similarly, the rescission of a resolution to share work with an unemployed member, where the evidence showed that his work was so bad that

---

[5] 29 U.S.C. § 412 (1970).

[6] LMRDA § 103, 29 U.S.C. § 413 (1970).

[7] Tomko v. Hilbert, 288 F.2d 625, 47 L.R.R.M. 2812 (3d Cir. 1961).

[8] Bougie v. Carpenters Dist. Council, 67 L.R.R.M. 2402 (N.D. Ind. 1968).

no employer would have accepted him, was held not to amount to discipline. The Third Circuit Court of Appeals characterized the action as a "mere 'slap on the wrist.' "[9]

Along the same line, when a union's action regarding a member is taken to comply with the terms of a collective bargaining agreement or with a legal requirement, it is not viewed as discipline. For example, a union's refusal to refer a member for a job for which he does not qualify under the terms of the collective bargaining agreement is not discipline.[10] The member suffers no detriment since, even if he had been referred to the employer, he would be ineligible for the position. Likewise, a union's refusal, in compliance with the decision of a National Labor Relations Board examiner, to allow supervisory employee-members to vote in an election is not viewed as discipline.[11] Since they have no legal right to vote, they suffer no detriment when not allowed to vote.

On the other hand, if a member suffers a detriment, an action may be characterized as discipline even if it was undertaken for a proper administrative reason and no harm was intended.[12] For example, the revocation of a local's charter, even if done for a legitimate reason, is discipline if it results in members losing basic membership rights.[13] Basic membership rights include the right to belong to a local,[14] the right to run for office in a local, and the right to retain the undiluted power of one's vote.[15]

The third general requirement of discipline is that it be judicial, rather than legislative, in nature. A rule that is adopted, if prospective in nature, will not be considered to be discipline.

---

[9] Rekant v. Shochtay-Gasos, Local 446, 320 F.2d 271, 277, 53 L.R.R.M. 2574, 2579 (3d Cir. 1963).

[10] Figueroa v. Maritime Union, 342 F.2d 400, 58 L.R.R.M. 2619 (2d Cir. 1965).

[11] Local 13410, UMW v. UMW of Am., 475 F.2d 906, 82 L.R.R.M. 2206 (D.C. Cir. 1973).

[12] Pittman v. United Bhd. of Carpenters, 251 F. Supp. 323, 62 L.R.R.M. 2784 (M.D. Fla. 1966).

[13] *Id.*

[14] Calabrese v. United Ass'n of Plumbers, 211 F. Supp. 609, 52 L.R.R.M. 2022 (D.N.J. 1962), *aff'd per curiam*, 324 F.2d 955, 54 L.R.R.M. 2780 (3d Cir. 1963).

[15] Pittman v. United Bhd. of Carpenters, 251 F. Supp. 323, 62 L.R.R.M. 2784 (M.D. Fla. 1966).

In one case, a union adopted a prospective rule, obviously aimed at only one member of the local. The rule denied arbitration rights to those members (there was only one) with excessive absenteeism. The court held that since it was a prospective rule, not punishing any past behavior, it was not discipline for the union to adopt and enforce such a rule.[16]

The three basic elements, then, of discipline are that it be action by the union or its officers engaged in their official capacity; it must cause some detriment to the member; and it must be a judicial, not a legislative action.

Some courts have determined that since the Act is designed to deal with a member's relationship with the union, only actions which affect the member's status within the union are discipline.[17] The majority of the courts which have dealt with the issue, however, have concluded that union action which affects a member's employment may also be discipline. This is the more realistic view. The Act was designed to protect members from improper union actions. By interpreting it liberally in this area, the legislative intent is more likely to be fulfilled. If it were construed narrowly, unions would be able to impose sanctions on members by affecting a member's employment opportunities without providing Section 101(a)(5) safeguards. Following the liberal interpretation, the courts have held that blacklisting a member,[18] interfering with employment opportunities,[19] refusing to prosecute arbitrable grievances,[20] refusing

---

[16] Scovile v. Watson, 338 F.2d 678, 57 L.R.R.M. 2513 (7th Cir. 1964), *cert. denied*, 380 U.S. 963, 58 L.R.R.M. 2768 (1965).

[17] Lucas v. Kenny, 220 F. Supp. 188, 53 L.R.R.M. 2949 (N.D. Ill. 1963); Beauchamp v. Weeks, 48 L.R.R.M. 3048 (S.D. Cal. 1961); Allen v. Armored Car Chauffeurs, Local 820, 185 F. Supp. 492, 45 L.R.R.M. 3067 (D.N.J. 1960).

[18] Detroy v. American Guild of Variety Artists, 286 F.2d 75, 47 L.R.R.M. 2452 (2d Cir.), *cert. denied*, 366 U.S. 929, 48 L.R.R.M. 2205 (1961); Burris v. Teamsters Union, 224 F. Supp. 277, 54 L.R.R.M. 2750 (W.D.N.C. 1963).

[19] Figueroa v. Maritime Union, 342 F.2d 400, 58 L.R.R.M. 2619 (2d Cir. 1965).

[20] Scovile v. Watson, 338 F.2d 678, 57 L.R.R.M. 2513 (7th Cir. 1964), *cert. denied*, 380 U.S. 963, 58 L.R.R.M. 2768 (1965); Catanzaro v. Soft Drink Workers, Local 812, 65 L.R.R.M. 2092 (E.D.N.Y. 1967); Broomer v. Schultz, 239 F. Supp. 699 (E.D. Pa. 1965), *aff'd per curiam*, 356 F.2d 984 (3d Cir. 1966).

to refer a member for employment,[21] and causing an employer to discharge a member [22] may, in some circumstances, constitute discipline.

The courts do recognize, however, that the unions must be free to make policy decisions in their dealings with employers. Hence, not every refusal to pursue a grievance [23] or every refusal to refer a member for hiring [24] is considered discipline. A union must be free to make policy decisions concerning its relationships with employers, in order to serve the common good of the union members. A refusal to pursue a grievance may be part of an overall bargaining strategy. A refusal to refer an unqualified member to an employer may serve the union in the long run. The union is free to make such decisions based on policy considerations. It may not, however, make such decisions for the purpose of disciplining members without granting them their Section 101(a)(5) rights.

WHO IS PROTECTED?

Section 101(a)(5) is designed to protect members of labor organizations. Section 3(o) of the Act defines the term "member." [25] It has been held that only union members are protected

---

[21] Figueroa v. Maritime Union, 342 F.2d 400, 58 L.R.R.M. 2619 (2d Cir. 1965).

[22] Duncan v. Peninsula Shipbuilders Ass'n, 394 F.2d 237, 68 L.R.R.M. 2135 (4th Cir. 1968); Gross v. Kennedy, 183 F. Supp. 750, 46 L.R.R.M. 2169 (S.D.N.Y. 1960).

[23] Scovile v. Watson, 338 F.2d 678, 57 L.R.R.M. 2513 (7th Cir. 1964), *cert. denied*, 380 U.S. 963, 58 L.R.R.M. 2768 (1965).

[24] Figueroa v. Maritime Union, 342 F.2d 400, 58 L.R.R.M. 2619 (2d Cir. 1965).

[25] 29 U.S.C. § 402(o) (1970) states:

"Member" or "member in good standing," when used in reference to a labor organization, includes any person who has fulfilled the requirements for membership in such an organization, and who has neither voluntarily withdrawn from membership nor has been expelled or suspended from membership after appropriate proceedings consistent with the lawful provisions of the constitution and bylaws of such organization.

Moynahan v. Pari-Mutuel Employees, Local 280, 317 F.2d 209, 53 L.R.R.M. 2154 (9th Cir.), *cert. denied*, 375 U.S. 911, 54 L.R.R.M. 2611 (1963) held that this section does not limit the right of a union to choose its members. Apparently, one of the requirements referred to in Section 3(o) is that the union must have allowed the person to join.

by Title I.[26] Since a person who has been suspended from a union is not a member, he is not protected by Title I.[27] It follows that if the person has been expelled, he is no longer entitled to Title I rights.

The scope of protection that Section 101(a)(5) affords officers and employees of labor unions is not clear. Such personnel may be removed from their positions for official misconduct without the procedural safeguards the Act guarantees to rank and file members.[28] The Conference Report notes:

> . . . the prohibition on suspension without observing certain safeguards applies only to suspension of membership in the union; it does not refer to suspension of a member's status as an officer in the union.[29]

The late John F. Kennedy, then a Senate conferee, suggested that the distinction may be based on the need for immediate action:

> [A]ll the conferees agreed that this provision does not relate to suspension or removal from a union office. Often this step must be taken summarily to prevent dissipation or misappropriation of funds.[30]

This line of reasoning also justifies the immediate removal of a union employee for his misconduct as an official.

It does not necessarily follow from this rationale that no removal from office or employment is subject to Section 101(a) (5). When the removal is for official misconduct, speed is necessary, and the lack of safeguards is acceptable. When, however, the removal is based on the person's actions as a union member rather than as a union official, the need for summary action is much less clear. There is no more need summarily to discipline such a member than there is to do so with any other member. The courts have been faced with having to determine if an official is entitled to safeguards for his actions as a member.

---

[26] Perkins v. Maritime Union, 67 L.R.R.M. 2735 (S.D.N.Y. 1968); Johnson v. Local 58, IBEW, 181 F. Supp. 734, 45 L.R.R.M. 2687 (E.D. Mich. 1960).

[27] Stone v. Local 29, Boilermakers, 262 F. Supp. 961, 64 L.R.R.M. 2274 (D. Mass. 1967).

[28] Burton v. Packinghouse Workers, Local 12, 199 F. Supp. 138, 49 L.R.R.M. 2122 (D. Kan. 1961); Hamilton v. Guinan, 199 F. Supp. 562, 49 L.R.R.M. 2356 (S.D.N.Y. 1961).

[29] H.R. REP. No. 1147, 86th Cong., 1st Sess. 31 (1959).

[30] 105 CONG. REC. 17,899 (1959).

When a union member takes on an official capacity as a union officer or employee, should he retain his right, as a union member, not to be disciplined for his actions as a member without Section 101(a)(5) safeguards? Such an interpretation of the law would protect the member for his acts as a member, and the union from the member for his misconduct as an official. If the act were performed by the official while acting as an individual union member, he would be entitled to the same protection as everyone else. If the act were official misconduct, summary action would be allowed. Although this approach requires that the union determine how, in fact, the action is taken, as a member's action or as an official's action—it seems to be the approach that would best balance the two competing interests. Unfortunately, this argument has been rejected by the various circuit courts of appeal that have considered it.[31] They have held, based on the legislative history, that Section 101(a)(5) does not apply to any suspension or removal of a member from an official position. The Ninth Circuit Court of Appeals explained its reading of the legislative history:

> In deference to the "patent legislative intent" it has been held with virtual unanimity that section 101(a)(5) does not apply to removal or suspension from union office. We think these decisions are correct. Furthermore, we think it makes no difference what the reason for the summary removal may have been. Congress's primary concern was that section 101(a)(5) should not bar summary removal of union officials suspected of malfeasance, but the means Congress chose to accomplish its purpose was to wholly exclude suspension or removal from union office from the category of union action to which section 101(a)(5) applied.[32]

Thus, despite contrary opinions, Section 101(a)(5) does not seem to protect union officials from suspension or removal from office.

This result does not, however, mean that a union official receives no protection from the Act. If the action against the official does more than merely strip him of his official position,

[31] Wood v. Dennis, 489 F.2d 849, 84 L.R.R.M. 2662 (7th Cir. 1972), *cert. denied,* 415 U.S. 960, 85 L.R.R.M. 2530 (1974); Martire v. Laborers' Local 1058, 410 F.2d 32, 70 L.R.R.M. 3378 (3d Cir.), *cert. denied,* 396 U.S. 903, 72 L.R.R.M. 2658 (1969); Grand Lodge, IAM v. King, 335 F.2d 340, 56 L.R.R.M. 2639 (9th Cir.), *cert. denied,* 379 U.S. 920, 57 L.R.R.M. 2512 (1964); Sheridan v. Carpenters, Local 626, 306 F.2d 152, 50 L.R.R.M. 2637 (3d Cir. 1962).

[32] Grand Lodge, IAM v. King, 335 F.2d 340, 342-43, 56 L.R.R.M. 2639, 2640 (9th Cir. 1965), *cert. denied,* 379 U.S. 920, 57 L.R.R.M. 2512 (1964).

Section 101 (a) (5) will again be applicable. Also, if the action against the official is based on his exercising any of his rights guaranteed by Title I of the Act, Section 609 may offer the official some protection.

If, in the course of removing an official from his position, other sanctions may result, Section 101 (a) (5) will once more offer the member protection from those other sanctions. This is because any discipline which affects the official's status, not as a union official but as a union member, is allowed only when the proper procedural safeguards are observed. For example, if the official may be expelled from the union [33] or barred from holding office,[34] he is entitled to the safeguards that Section 101 (a) (5) provides.

Section 609 of the Act may also afford an officer some protection for his acts as a union member. It states:

> It shall be unlawful for any labor organization, or any officer, agent, shop steward, or other representative of a labor organization, or any employee thereof to fine, suspend, expel, or otherwise discipline any of its members for exercising any right to which he is entitled under the provisions of this Act. The provisions in section 102 shall be applicable in the enforcement of this section.[35]

In two cases, the Third Circuit Court of Appeals has held that unseating an officer because of his conduct as a member is not discipline under, and hence not protected by, Section 609.[36] The Seventh and Ninth Circuit Courts of Appeal, however, have reached the opposite conclusion.[37] As the Ninth Circuit explained:

---

[33] Lewis v. Federation of State, County, and Municipal Employees, 407 F.2d 1185, 70 L.R.R.M. 2707 (3d Cir.), *cert. denied,* 396 U.S. 866, 73 L.R.R.M. 2236 (1969).

[34] Schonfeld v. Penza, 477 F.2d 899, 83 L.R.R.M. 2020 (2d Cir. 1973); Martire v. Laborers' Local 1058, 410 F.2d 32, 70 L.R.R.M. 3378 (3d Cir.), *cert. denied,* 396 U.S. 903, 72 L.R.R.M. 2658 (1969).

[35] 29 U.S.C. § 529 (1970).

[36] Martire v. Laborers' Local 1058, 410 F.2d 32, 70 L.R.R.M. 3378 (3d Cir.), *cert. denied,* 396 U.S. 903, 72 L.R.R.M. 2658 (1969); Sheridan v. Carpenters, Local 626, 306 F.2d 152, 50 L.R.R.M. 2637 (3d Cir. 1962).

[37] Wood v. Dennis, 489 F.2d 849, 84 L.R.R.M. 2662 (7th Cir. 1972), *cert. denied,* 415 U.S. 960, 85 L.R.R.M. 2530 (1974); Grand Lodge, IAM v. King, 335 F.2d 340, 56 L.R.R.M. 2639 (9th Cir.), *cert. denied,* 379 U.S. 920, 57 L.R.R.M. 2512 (1964).

> Sections 101(a)(5) and 609 have wholly different purposes, and the difference is such as to satisfy us that although Congress did not intend the words "otherwise discipline" to include removal from union office in section 101(a)(5), it did intend the words to include such action in section 609.[38]

The court went on to point out that Section 609 has nothing to do with summary discipline. The legislative restriction on Section 101(a)(5) should therefore not apply to Section 609. To a large extent, this reading restores protection to union officers and employees for their actions taken as members. If such actions are protected by Title I, then the officers and employees are still protected from discipline.

In sum, as the law stands, a union officer or employee may be suspended or removed from office for any reason without the procedural safeguards provided by Section 101(a)(5). A more appropriate view would limit this right of removal to instances involving official misconduct, but the circuit courts of appeal have held that only if additional discipline is contemplated must the safeguards be observed. The circuit courts of appeal are split as to whether Section 609 may restrict suspension or removal from office when Title I rights are involved. Since protection of union members is the Act's purpose, the preferable interpretation of Section 609 would restrict the right to affect a member's official status, thus guaranteeing the member the most protection under the Act.

WRITTEN SPECIFIC CHARGES

Section 101(a)(5)(A) requires that the member being tried be "served with written specific charges." These charges must be, in Senator McClellan's words, "specific enough to inform the accused member of the offense he has allegedly committed." [39] The courts have interpreted the phrase to mean that the charges must give the member ". . . the information needed to conduct a meaningful investigation and prepare a defense." [40]

---

[38] Grand Lodge, IAM v. King, 335 F.2d 340, 345, 56 L.R.R.M. 2639, 2642 (9th Cir.), *cert. denied*, 379 U.S. 920, 57 L.R.R.M. 2512 (1964).

[39] LABOR-MANAGEMENT REFORM LEGISLATION, *Hearings before a Joint Sub-Committee of the House Committee on Education and Labor*, 86th Cong., 1st Sess., pt. 5, at 2285 (1959).

[40] Gleason v. Chain Service Restaurant, 422 F.2d 342, 343, 73 L.R.R.M. 2781, 2783 (2d Cir. 1970).

The courts have recognized that in many cases union officers, untrained in the law, will be formulating the charges. As a result, it has been stated that:

> We do not expect union officials to frame their charges and specifications technically as formal legal pleadings. However, we do require that they be so drafted as to inform a member with reasonable particularity of the details of the charge. . . .[41]

A mere listing of the section of the union constitution or bylaws that the member is accused of violating is not sufficiently specific.[42] The charges must also include the factual basis [43] and some statement informing the accused of the time, place, and circumstances of the alleged offense.[44] The charges will be considered specific enough, even if they do not disclose the names of the people involved in the incident, if they are sufficiently precise so that the accused knows what the charges are.[45] If, however, they are so general that the accused would not be able to ascertain the gravamen of the charges unless he were, in fact, guilty, then they are not specific enough.[46]

It was originally thought that a union could bring charges against a member only for violating existing provisions in the union's constitution and bylaws.[47] Additionally, it was believed that such "penal provisions in union constitutions must be strictly construed." [48] The Supreme Court, however, in *Boiler-*

---

[41] Jacques v. Longshoremen's Local 1418, 246 F. Supp. 857, 859-60, 60 L.R.R.M. 2320, 2321 (E.D. La. 1965), *aff'd per curiam*, 404 F.2d 703, 69 L.R.R.M. 2983 (5th Cir. 1968).

[42] Caraballo v. Operadores de Ponce, 55 L.R.R.M. 2787 (D.P.R. 1964).

[43] Magelssen v. Plasterers, Local 518, 233 F. Supp. 459, 57 L.R.R.M. 2444 (W.D. Mo. 1964).

[44] Jacques v. Longshoremen's Local 1418, 246 F. Supp. 857, 60 L.R.R.M. 2320 (E.D. La. 1965), *aff'd per curiam*, 404 F.2d 703, 69 L.R.R.M. 2983 (5th Cir. 1968).

[45] Null v. Carpenters Dist. Council, 239 F. Supp. 809, 59 L.R.R.M. 2645 (S.D. Tex. 1965); Carroll v. Musicians Local 802, 235 F. Supp. 161, 52 L.R.R.M. 2950 (S.D.N.Y. 1963); Vars v. International Bhd. of Boilermakers, 215 F. Supp. 943, 52 L.R.R.M. 2872 (D. Conn.), *aff'd*, 320 F.2d 576, 53 L.R.R.M. 2690 (2d Cir. 1963).

[46] Gleason v. Chain Service Restaurant, 422 F.2d 342, 73 L.R.R.M. 2781 (2d Cir. 1970).

[47] Simmons v. Avisco, Local 713, Textile Workers, 350 F.2d 1012, 60 L.R.R.M. 2131 (4th Cir. 1965).

[48] International Bhd. of Boilermakers v. Braswell, 388 F.2d 193, 198, 67 L.R.R.M. 2250, 2254 (5th Cir.), *cert. denied*, 391 U.S. 935, 68 L.R.R.M.

makers v. Hardeman,[49] examined the legislative history of the Act and concluded that a union may discipline its members for conduct "not proscribed by written rules at all."[50] It held that:

[Section 101(a)(5)(A)] gives courts no warrant to scrutinize the union regulations in order to determine whether particular conduct may be punished at all.[51]

Likewise, the Court held that it is not proper for a court to examine the scope of union rules to see whether conduct falls within it.[52]

The Court explained its refusal to require written rules of definite scope by reference to the legislative history of Section 101(a)(5). As that section was originally proposed by Senator McClellan, discipline would have been forbidden "except for breach of a published written rule of [the union]."[53] Three days after Senator McClellan's amendment was accepted, a substitute amendment offered by Senator Kuchel was adopted. It transformed Senator McClellan's amendment, in relevant part, to the current language of Section 101(a)(5). This was the result of some objections to the language of Senator McClellan's amendment. For example, John F. Kennedy, then a senator, had objected:

In the case of . . . the . . . official who bribed a judge, unless there were a specific prohibition against bribery of judicial officers written into the constitution of the union, then no union could take disciplinary action against [an] officer or member guilty of bribery.[54]

The Court pointed out that Congress did understand that the substitute amendment made substantive changes in Senator McClellan's proposal.[55] After the Kuchel amendment passed the

---

2283 (1968), *quoting* Allen v. Theatrical Employees, 338 F.2d 309, 316, 57 L.R.R.M. 2368, 2374 (5th Cir. 1964).

[49] 401 U.S. 233, 76 L.R.R.M. 2542 (1971).

[50] *Id.* at 244, 76 L.R.R.M. at 2546.

[51] *Id.* at 245, 76 L.R.R.M. at 2546.

[52] *Id.* at 244-45, 76 L.R.R.M. 2546.

[53] 105 CONG. REC. 6476, 6492-93 (1959).

[54] 105 CONG. REC. 6476, 6491 (1959).

[55] 401 U.S. at 243, 76 L.R.R.M. at 2546.

Senate, Senator Goldwater explained it to the House Committee on Labor and Education:

> . . . [T]he bill of rights in the Senate bill requires that the union member be served with written specific charges prior to any disciplinary proceedings but it does not require that these charges, to be valid, must be based on activity that the union had proscribed prior to the union member having engaged in such activity.[56]

Senator McClellan gave testimony to the same effect.[57] Given this legislative history, the Court was correct in its interpretation of the law.

Despite the seeming validity of the Court's interpretation, its result is unfortunate. In most situations, the courts recognize that ex post facto laws and rules are unjust. It is not fair to discipline a person for conduct that he did not know and could not know was wrong. Unless there is an overriding policy justification, the abandonment of this concept by Congress and the Court is desirable.

The one policy justification that the Court offered does not seem valid. The Court emphasized the objection offered by the late Senator Kennedy—that without allowing ex post facto rules severe improper conduct might go unpunished. This objection, however, is unconvincing. If states and countries are able to formulate the laws required to govern large numbers of people and issues, it is not unreasonable to require unions also to specify their rules. In other areas, governing bodies have been doing so for years. Unions, too, should be required to formulate their rules for their members to see and to understand. Granted, while every possible infraction cannot be described, or even listed, guidelines containing specific examples of prohibited conduct could be provided.

A second policy, if enacted, would minimize federal government interference in the internal affairs of unions; this policy may have influenced Congress but was not considered by the Court. When the right of the individual member to know what conduct can cause him to be fined, expelled from his union, or otherwise disciplined is undermined, the federal government, in this instance, should intervene in the internal affairs of unions.

Given the legislative history of Section 101(a)((5), the Supreme Court probably did interpret the section as Congress

---

[56] LABOR-MANAGEMENT REFORM LEGISLATION, *supra* note 39, pt. 4 at 1595.

[57] 401 U.S. at 244, 76 L.R.R.M. at 2546.

intended. Unfortunately, however, the reasons for not allowing ex post facto laws ought to apply to unions as well as to other governing bodies. There are no counterbalancing policy reasons for allowing unions to make ex post facto laws. An amendment to Section 101(a)(5), forbidding discipline except for breach of a published, written rule of the union, seems appropriate. Currently, only state laws offer members protection in this area. The Supreme Court, in a footnote in *Hardeman*, did recognize that state law may go farther.[58]

Since a member must be served with specific written charges, it is improper for a union tribunal to try a member on charges not specified in the notice.[59] If the written charges with which a member is served are not specific enough, the union may remedy the defect thereafter by serving him with a bill of particulars. In one case, when the union supplied a bill of particulars at the member's request, the court found the charges were sufficiently specific.[60] Whether the union offers or the member requests the details of the charge, the law is satisfied as long as the member becomes fully informed of the charges in writing. It is not, of course, the member's responsibility to secure a bill of particulars.

> The [union] argues that the [member] through his own efforts could have obtained charges sufficiently specific to withstand judicial review. Under the statute it is not the duty of an accused member to secure a written notice of the specific charges; it is the duty of the union to give such notice in the accusation. . . .[61]

---

[58] *Id.* at 244 n. 11, 76 L.R.R.M. at 2546 n. 11.

State law, in many circumstances, may go farther. *See* Summers, *The Law of Union Discipline: What the Courts Do in Fact*, 70 YALE L.J. 175 (1960). But Congress, which preserved state law remedies by § 103 of the LMRDA, 29 U.S.C. § 413, was well aware that even the broad language of Senator McClellan's original proposal was more limited in scope than much state law. *See* 105 CONG. REC. 6481-6489.

[59] Allen v. Theatrical Employees, 338 F.2d 309, 57 L.R.R.M. 2368 (5th Cir. 1964).

[60] Rosen v. Painters Dist. Council 9, 198 F. Supp. 46, 48 L.R.R.M. 2721 (S.D.N.Y. 1961), *appeal dismissed*, 326 F.2d 400, 55 L.R.R.M. 2169 (2d Cir. 1964).

[61] Magelssen v. Plasterers, Local 518, 233 F. Supp. 459, 57 L.R.R.M. 2444 (W.D. Mo. 1964).

REASONABLE TIME TO PREPARE A DEFENSE

Section 101(a)(5)(B) requires that the union give the member "a reasonable time to prepare his defense." No per se rules have been adopted specifying which time periods are or are not acceptable. Each case must be examined in the context of its own circumstances to determine what time period is "reasonable."

Generally, eight days or less have been found to be too short a time period.[62] Although this is not a per se rule, it may be that the courts view such a short time period as inherently suspect. It may be, therefore, the union's responsibility to demonstrate that the time period gave the accused sufficient time to understand the charge, to investigate, to secure counsel and witnesses, to plan a strategy, and otherwise to prepare for trial.

At the other end of the spectrum, twenty-one days or more have generally been found to be a reasonable period.[63] Again, this is not a per se rule. In the eyes of the courts, however, such a time period may give rise to a presumption of regularity. The courts may, therefore, place the burden on the accused member to show that he was unable to prepare for trial in three weeks.

The reasonableness of the allotted time period (between eight and twenty-one days) varies with the individual circumstances of the case. One of the circumstances the courts have examined is the time period the union constitution provides. This period is apparently that which the union itself has determined is reason-

---

[62] Simmons v. Avisco, Local 713, Textile Workers, 350 F.2d 1012, 1017 n. 9, 60 L.R.R.M. 2131, 2134 n. 9 (4th Cir. 1965); Jacques v. Longshoremen's Local 1418, 246 F. Supp. 857, 60 L.R.R.M. 2320 (E.D. La. 1965), *aff'd per curiam,* 404 F.2d 703, 69 L.R.R.M. 2983 (5th Cir. 1968); Caraballo v. Operadores de Ponce, 55 L.R.R.M. 2787 (D.P.R. 1964); Deluhery v. Marine Cooks and Stewards Union, 211 F. Supp. 529, 51 L.R.R.M. 2682 (S.D. Cal. 1962).

[63] Jacques v. Longshoremen's Local 1418, 246 F. Supp. 857, 60 L.R.R.M. 2320 (E.D. La. 1965), *aff'd per curiam,* 404 F.2d 703, 69 L.R.R.M. 2983 (5th Cir. 1968); Null v. Carpenters Dist. Council, 239 F. Supp. 809, 59 L.R.R.M. 2645 (S.D. Tex. 1965); Carroll v. Musicians Local 802, 235 F. Supp. 161, 52 L.R.R.M. 2950 (S.D.N.Y. 1963); Rosen v. Painters Dist. Council 9, 198 F. Supp. 46, 48 L.R.R.M. 2721 (S.D.N.Y. 1961), *appeal dismissed,* 326 F.2d 400, 55 L.R.R.M. 2169 (2d Cir. 1964).

able.[64] At a minimum, the union should give the accused the amount of time required by its rules.[65] Other factors that have been considered by various courts include the adequacy of the written notice,[66] the availability of assistance from other members or from an attorney,[67] the granting of postponements,[68] and the prejudicial effect of the time allowed.[69]

---

[64] Various unions provide different time periods during which the accused is permitted to prepare his defense. *E.g.*, the *Constitution of the International Ladies' Garment Workers' Union*, Art. 22, § 3 (1971) provides:

> Section 1. Notice and time of trial
> The secretary of the appropriate trial committee shall give the accused and the accuser written notice of the time and place of the trial hearing. Such hearing shall be held between five days and one month after such charges are received by the two parties.

The *Constitution of the International Brotherhood of Teamsters, Chauffeurs, Warehousemen and Helpers of America*, Art. XIX, § 1(b) (1971) provides:

> . . . the accused shall be required to stand trial at the time and place designated, which shall not be less than ten (10) days from the date the charges are served upon the accused. . . .

The *Constitution and By-Laws, Amalgamated Clothing Workers of America*, Art. XI, § 3 (1974) provides:

> Section 3. Proceedings under this Article may be initiated by any member of the Amalgamated by filing written charges, specifying the acts or conduct with which the accused is charged, with the secretary-treasurer of the appropriate local union or joint board or with the General Secretary-Treasurer, as the case may be. The secretary with whom such charges are filed shall promptly transmit a copy thereof to the accused at his or her last known address together with written notice of the time and place of the hearing thereon, which shall be held not less than five (5) days after the date of the notice.

[65] Jacques v. Longshoremen's Local 1418, 246 F. Supp. 857, 60 L.R.R.M. 2320 (E.D. La. 1965), *aff'd per curiam*, 404 F.2d 703, 69 L.R.R.M. 2983 (5th Cir. 1968); Vars v. International Bhd. of Boilermakers, 215 F. Supp. 943, 52 L.R.R.M. 2872 (D. Conn.), *aff'd*, 320 F.2d 576, 53 L.R.R.M. 2690 (2d Cir. 1963).

[66] Rosen v. Painters Dist. Council 9, 198 F. Supp. 46, 48 L.R.R.M. 2721 (S.D.N.Y. 1961), *appeal dismissed*, 326 F.2d 400, 55 L.R.R.M. 2169 (2d Cir. 1964).

[67] Vars v. International Bhd. of Boilermakers, 215 F. Supp. 943, 52 L.R.R.M. 2872 (D. Conn.), *aff'd*, 320 F.2d 576, 53 L.R.R.M. 2690 (2d Cir. 1963); Rosen v. Painters Dist. Council 9, 198 F. Supp. 46, 48 L.R.R.M. 2721 (S.D.N.Y. 1961), *appeal dismissed*, 326 F.2d 400, 55 L.R.R.M. 2169 (2d Cir. 1964).

[68] Caraballo v. Operadores de Ponce, 55 L.R.R.M. 2787 (D.P.R. 1964); Rosen v. Painters Dist. Council 9, 198 F. Supp. 46, 48 L.R.R.M. 2721 (S.D.N.Y. 1961), *appeal dismissed*, 326 F.2d 400, 55 L.R.R.M. 2169 (2d Cir. 1964).

[69] Burke v. International Bhd. of Boilermakers, 302 F. Supp. 1345, 72 L.R.R.M. 2749 (N.D. Cal. 1967), *aff'd per curiam*, 417 F.2d 1063, 72 L.R.R.M.

Logically, if the union first serves a member with written charges that are not specific enough, and later gives him a bill of particulars, the time period should start when the member receives the specifics of the charge.[70]

FULL AND FAIR HEARING

Section 101 (a) (5) (C) guarantees each member a "full and fair hearing." Congress left the interpretation of this phrase to the courts. Although in some areas such hearing requirements resemble criminal due process, more often they are closer to the due process requirements of an administrative agency.

Presumption of Innocence

The first requirement of a full and fair hearing is that the accused be assumed innocent until proven guilty. The burden of proof must initially be on the party in the prosecutorial function. For a union to presume a member guilty until proven innocent would certainly run counter to a court's sense of justice and fair play. Thus, where a union tried a member under Roberts' Rules of Order and did not afford him this presumption, the court found a violation of the Act.[71]

Right to Present Evidence

In order for a trial to be fair, the accused must be allowed to present his side of the story. He therefore has the right to be present,[72] to speak on his own behalf,[73] to call wit-

---

2573 (9th Cir. 1969) ; Vars v. International Bhd. of Boilermakers, 215 F. Supp. 943, 52 L.R.R.M. 2872 (D. Conn.), *aff'd*, 320 F.2d 576, 53 L.R.R.M. 2690 (2d Cir. 1963).

[70] Rosen v. Painters Dist. Council 9, 198 F. Supp. 46, 48 L.R.R.M. 2721 (S.D.N.Y. 1961), *appeal dismissed*, 326 F.2d 400, 55 L.R.R.M. 2169 (2d Cir. 1964).

[71] Nelson v. Painters, Local 386, 47 L.R.R.M. 2441 (D. Minn. 1961).

[72] Kiepura v. Local 1091, Steelworkers, 358 F. Supp. 987, 84 L.R.R.M. 2847 (N.D. Ill. 1973) ; Hart v. Carpenters, Local 1292, 341 F. Supp. 1266, 80 L.R.R.M. 2188 (E.D.N.Y. 1972), *aff'd per curiam*, 497 F.2d 401, 86 L.R.R.M. 2447 (2d Cir. 1974) ; Anderson v. Brotherhood of Carpenters, 53 L.R.R.M. 2793 (D. Minn. 1963) ; Allen v. Iron Workers, Local 92, 47 L.R.R.M. 2214 (N.D. Ala. 1960).

[73] *See, e.g.*, Parks v. IBEW, 314 F.2d 886, 52 L.R.R.M. 2281 (4th Cir.), *cert. denied*, 372 U.S. 976, 52 L.R.R.M. 2943 (1963) ; Detroy v. American

nesses,[74] and to present evidence.[75] Without these rights, the accused would have no way to refute properly the charges and evidence against him.

Right to Confrontation and Cross-Examination

In addition to introducing his own evidence, an accused must have the right to confront witnesses who testify against him and the right to cross-examine them.[76] This is because it is an adversary hearing. The courts recognize that one of the most effective ways to impeach a witness and to elicit the truth is by cross-examination. Therefore, the accused must be allowed not only to present his own evidence but also to impeach the union's witnesses in order to have a "full and fair hearing."

Waiver of Rights

If a member fails to appear at his trial, or if he fails to exercise his right to present evidence and to cross-examine adverse witnesses, he is deemed to have waived these rights.[77] Since participating in the trial does not necessarily waive fundamental objections which the member may have as to the specificity of the charges, the time that he was given to prepare

---

Guild of Variety Artists, 286 F.2d 75, 47 L.R.R.M. 2452 (2d Cir.), *cert. denied*, 366 U.S. 929, 48 L.R.R.M. 2205 (1961); Yochim v. Caputo, 51 L.R.R.M. 2516 (S.D.N.Y. 1962).

[74] Kiepura v. Local 1091, Steelworkers, 358 F. Supp. 987, 84 L.R.R.M. 2847 (N.D. Ill. 1973); Kuykendall v. Carpenters, Local 1763, 56 L.R.R.M. 2455 (D. Wyo. 1964); Yochim v. Caputo, 51 L.R.R.M. 2516 (S.D.N.Y. 1962); Nelson v. Painters, Local 386, 47 L.R.R.M. 2441 (D. Minn. 1961).

[75] Parks v. IBEW, 314 F.2d 886, 52 L.R.R.M. 2281 (4th Cir.), *cert. denied*, 372 U.S. 976, 52 L.R.R.M. 2943 (1963); Kiepura v. Local 1091, Steelworkers, 358 F. Supp. 987, 84 L.R.R.M. 2847 (N.D. Ill. 1973); Air Line Stewards, Local 550 v. Transport Workers Union, 55 L.R.R.M. 2711 (N.D. Ill. 1963), *rev'd on other grounds*, 334 F.2d 805, 56 L.R.R.M. 2752 (7th Cir. 1964), *cert. denied*, 379 U.S. 972, 58 L.R.R.M. 2192 (1965).

[76] Parks v. IBEW, 314 F.2d 886, 52 L.R.R.M. 2281 (4th Cir.), *cert. denied*, 372 U.S. 976, 52 L.R.R.M. 2943 (1963); Kiepura v. Local 1091, Steelworkers, 358 F. Supp. 987, 84 L.R.R.M. 2847 (N.D. Ill. 1973); Telephone Workers, Local 2 v. International Bhd. of Tel. Workers, 261 F. Supp. 433, 64 L.R.R.M. 2029 (D. Mass. 1966); Anderson v. Brotherhood of Carpenters, 53 L.R.R.M. 2793 (D. Minn. 1963); Yochim v. Caputo, 51 L.R.R.M. 2516 (S.D.N.Y. 1962).

[77] Kuykendall v. Carpenters, Local 1763, 56 L.R.R.M. 2455 (D. Wyo. 1964).

his defense, or the way that the trial is conducted,[78] it will almost always be to the member's advantage to participate in the trial. There is always a chance that the member may be found not guilty by the union's trial body. If not, the member may still go to court with his objections concerning the charges, the time he was given to prepare his defense, or the trial procedures. In some circumstances, such as if the member objects to prejudice within the union trial body, participating in the trial may emphasize the union's improper conduct and improve the member's chances in court.

Right to Counsel

The provision in Section 101(a)(5)(C) for a full and fair hearing does not, apparently, include a right to have an attorney at the union trial.[79] The courts have held that the Sixth Amendment right to counsel "does not apply to hearings before labor unions." [80] There is, of course, no limitation on a member's right to seek a lawyer's advice outside the trial. Thus, even though the accused may not have his attorney present at the trial, the attorney may be an integral part of the defense. He may plan strategy, prepare witnesses, and generally do all of the work an attorney would normally do prior to trial. In addition, if the union uses an attorney in the prosecution of the case, the accused, in order to be on equal footing, is also entitled to one.[81] To allow the union to have professional help at the trial while denying similar aid to the accused would be inequitable. Unfortunately, the accused member's privilege of seeking

---

[78] Falcone v. Dantinne, 420 F.2d 1157, 73 L.R.R.M. 2208 (3d Cir. 1969).

[79] Smith v. Sheet Metal Workers Int'l Ass'n, 357 F. Supp. 1386 (E.D. Tenn. 1972); Buresch v. IBEW, Local 24, 343 F. Supp. 183, 77 L.R.R.M. 2932 (D. Md. 1971), aff'd per curiam, 460 F.2d 1405, 79 L.R.R.M. 2615 (4th Cir. 1972); Sawyers v. Grand Lodge, IAM, 279 F. Supp. 747, 67 L.R.R.M. 2375 (E.D. Mo. 1967); Cornelio v. Carpenters, Metropolitan Dist. Council, 243 F. Supp. 126, 59 L.R.R.M. 2722 (E.D. Pa. 1965), aff'd per curiam, 358 F.2d 728, 61 L.R.R.M. 2688 (3d Cir. 1966), cert. denied, 386 U.S. 975 (1967); Smith v. Teamsters, Local 467, 181 F. Supp. 14, 45 L.R.R.M. 2848 (S.D. Cal. 1960).

[80] Smith v. Teamsters, Local 467, 181 F. Supp. 14, 45 L.R.R.M. 2848 (S.D. Cal. 1960).

[81] See Air Line Stewards, Local 550 v. Transport Workers Union, 55 L.R.R.M. 2711 (N.D. Ill. 1963), rev'd on other grounds, 334 F.2d 805, 56 L.R.R.M. 2752 (7th Cir. 1964), cert. denied, 379 U.S. 972, 58 L.R.R.M. 2192 (1965).

legal assistance, whether for out-of-court preparation or for representation at the union trial, will often be overshadowed by the union's similar rights. The union almost certainly has legal issues arising periodically, and may have an attorney on its staff or on retainer. At least the union will have a working relationship with a lawyer. Additionally, the union will normally have adequate funds from which to pay an attorney for his time and advice. The accused member, on the other hand, is unlikely to have any working relationship with an attorney. Even if he does have an attorney to whom he can turn, the member may not be able to afford the attorney's fees.[82] Thus, the member, even when seeking professional advice, may find that the union has an initial advantage.

Even if a member has no right to professional counsel, he may have a right to be represented by another member before the union tribunal. Many unions guarantee their members this right in their constitutions.[83] Numerous courts have cited such

---

[82] *See also* the discussion on attorneys' fees in this chapter, *infra.* p. 81.

[83] *E.g.*, the *Constitution of the International Brotherhood of Teamsters, Chauffers, Warehousemen and Helpers of America,* Art. XIX, § 1(b) (1971) provides:

> The accused may select only a member of his Local Union to represent him in the presentation of his defense; and the charging party may select only a member of his Local Union to assist him in the presentation of the evidence in support of the charges. . . .

The *Constitution of the International Ladies' Garment Workers' Union,* Art. 22, § 3 (1971) provides:

> Section 3. Witnesses and representation
> The accused person shall at all trials have the right to question all witnesses who may testify against him and to call such witnesses and present such evidence in his defense as he may deem necessary. He may do so in person or by a representative who shall be a member in good standing but not a general officer of the I.L.G.W.U. The accuser shall have the right to be represented by a representative in the same way as the accused. However, where there is a joint trial of more than one person upon charges accusing them of participation in the same offense, or accusing them of similar offenses arising out of the same transaction, there shall be only one representative for all such accused persons, and such representative shall be chosen by agreement of all the accused. Similarly, in a trial upon charges preferred by more than one accuser, there shall be only one representative for all such accusers, and such representative shall be chosen by agreement of all the accusers.

The *Constitution and Bylaws, Amalgamated Clothing Workers of America,* Art. XI, § 4 (1974) provides:

> Section 4. Hearings shall be held by the executive board of the local union, by the joint board or its executive board, or by the General

a procedure approvingly.[84] At least where the union constitution provides for it, Section 101(a)(5) has been held to require a member to have the right to a lay counsel.[85]

The compromise of allowing the accused to have lay, but not professional, counsel attempts to strike a balance between the needs of the union and the member. From the union's point of view, allowing another member to serve as lay counsel provides for a trial in which the forum appears fair. In addition, the use of lay counsel prevents the risk of outsiders entering into an internal union dispute. From the member's point of view, the use of lay counsel allows the accused to have someone act for him before the union tribunal. This may be a valuable right since the lay counsel, who is not suspected of improper conduct, may be in a better position than the accused to elicit favorable testimony and to cross-examine adverse witnesses. A representative to help investigate the charges, plan the trial strategy, and conduct the trial may be a very valuable asset for the accused.

Even when the accused member has a lay counsel, however, he may find himself at a disadvantage when he and his "counsel" appear at the union trial. In many cases, the union member in the prosecutorial role is a professional union man—the local

---

Executive Board, as the case may be, or by a committee appointed by such board to report the evidence to it: provided that all decisions shall be made by such board. The accused shall have the right to appear at such hearings, produce and cross-examine witnesses and be represented by any member of the Amalgamated in good standing designated by him for that purpose.

The *Constitution of the Oil, Chemical and Atomic Workers International Union*, Art. XII, § 4 (1973) provides:

Section 4. No evidence shall be considered by the Investigating Committee or the Union except such as shall be offered at a hearing at which the accused shall have been notified and given a reasonable opportunity to be present. The accused shall be given every reasonable opportunity to be heard and to present evidence in his defense. He may be assisted by counsel of his own choosing selected from the membership of his Local Union, or he may waive any or all of the rights set forth herein.

[84] Cornelio v. Carpenters, Metropolitan Dist. Council, 243 F. Supp. 126, 59 L.R.R.M. 2722 (E.D. Pa. 1965), *aff'd per curiam*, 358 F.2d 728, 61 L.R.R.M. 2688 (3d Cir. 1966), *cert. denied*, 386 U.S. 975 (1967); Null v. Carpenters Dist. Council, 239 F. Supp. 809, 59 L.R.R.M. 2645 (S.D. Tex. 1965); Rosen v. Painters Dist. Council 9, 198 F. Supp. 46, 48 L.R.R.M. 2721 (S.D.N.Y. 1961), *appeal dismissed*, 326 F.2d 400, 55 L.R.R.M. 2169 (2d Cir. 1964).

[85] Nelson v. Painters, Local 386, 47 L.R.R.M. 2441 (D. Minn. 1961).

representative of the international union. He may have received training regarding the union's constitution and bylaws, and he may have had extensive experience in union disciplinary matters. In such a case, one cannot contend that denying both sides professional counsel puts them on equal footing. In this prospective, the importance of at least lay counsel is readily apparent.

If a right to lay counsel exists, every accused member should be allowed to choose his own representative. In the event that he is unable to do so, either because he does not know whom to pick or because no member is willing to help him voluntarily, the union should be required to provide one for him. Such appointed counsel would have an obligation to represent the accused in good faith. This, of course, could be a difficult right to secure in practice; the union ought to have the obligation of assuring this right. Thereby, the union could comply with Section 101 (a) (5) (C)'s requirement of a full and fair hearing.

Right to a Transcript

Prior to the enactment of the Landrum-Griffin Act, the accused had no right to require that a transcript of the union trial be made.[86] After the Act was passed, it was originally believed that Section 101 (a) (5) (C) required that a transcript be made.[87] A footnote in *Hardemann,* however, implies that a transcript is not required:

> Although a transcript was made of the union proceedings in the present case, we have no reason to believe that this is a universal practice.[88]

Unfortunately, the implication herein is that the union is not required to make a transcript of the trial. If there is to be any appellate review of the union trial either by the union's internal appellate bodies or by federal courts, a transcript is fundamental. Without a transcript, a reviewing body will find it exceedingly difficult to examine the tribunal's action for bias, to ensure that the verdict is supported by the evidence, and to ascer-

---

[86] Underwood v. Maloney, 152 F. Supp. 648, 40 L.R.R.M. 2329 (E.D. Pa. 1957), *rev'd on other grounds,* 256 F.2d 334, 41 L.R.R.M. 2795 (3d Cir. 1958), *cert. denied,* 358 U.S. 864, 42 L.R.R.M. 2830 (1958).

[87] Etelson and Smith, *Union Discipline Under the Landrum-Griffin Act,* 82 HARV. L. REV. 727, 750 (1969).

[88] 401 U.S. at 246, n. 15, 76 L.R.R.M. at 2547 n. 15.

tain if proper safeguards were provided at the trial. If a transcript were made, the reviewing body would be able to examine not only current testimony about the trial, but also an official written record made at the time of the trial. The Supreme Court's footnote was simply dictum, but the issue merits the Court's direct consideration at some time.

The only legitimate argument on hand against requiring a transcript of each union trial is that such transcripts are expensive. On the other hand, a verbatim record of the union trial body's proceedings might help ensure that the union's appellate bodies or the courts be able to determine whether an accused received a full and fair hearing. One equitable solution to the problem would require unions to tape record all union trials. The tape recording equipment is inexpensive; it would probably cost two hundred to three hundred dollars. If the member does appeal the conviction, the tape itself, rather than a transcript, might suffice. In those instances where a party determines that a transcript is needed, one could be made from the tape recording at that party's expense. If a record of the proceeding will not be needed, the tape may be erased and reused.

In two cases decided since the Supreme Court's dictum in *Hardeman,* district courts, in specific circumstances, have found that transcripts are required. In one case, the court held that when the union's constitution requires that a transcript be made, an accused is not given a full and fair trial unless the required transcript is made.[89] In the other case, the court held that if the accused offers to obtain and pay for a stenographer, he has the right to have a transcript made.[90] These cases do limit the impact of the Supreme Court's dictum in *Hardeman.* If a transcript is required, it will not be considered defective if immaterial statements are omitted.[91]

---

[89] Hart v. Carpenters, Local 1292, 341 F. Supp. 1266, 80 L.R.R.M. 2188 (E.D.N.Y. 1972), *aff'd per curiam,* 497 F.2d 401, 86 L.R.R.M. 2447 (2d Cir. 1974).

[90] Kiepura v. Local 1091, Steelworkers, 358 F. Supp. 987, 84 L.R.R.M. 2847 (N.D. Ill. 1973).

[91] Vars v. International Bhd. of Boilermakers, 215 F. Supp. 943, 52 L.R.R.M. 2872 (D. Conn.), *aff'd,* 320 F.2d 576, 53 L.R.R.M. 2690 (2d Cir. 1963).

Right to an Unbiased Tribunal

An obvious requirement in giving an accused member a full and fair hearing is that the union tribunal be impartial.[92] If a trial body is biased, an impartial review by an appellate body will not cure the defect.[93]

The members serving on the trial board should be disinterested in the outcome.[94] Thus, where members of trial boards were political opponents of the accused, the courts found that the boards were biased.[95] Likewise, when the person presiding signed the charges, when members of the trial body testified, and when members of the trial body were involved in the matters leading to the charges, a court found bias.[96] A full and fair hearing cannot be given when members of the trial board were directly or indirectly involved in the matter that gave rise to the charges.[97] In addition, if a member of the trial body has prejudged the case, there is bias.[98] The tribunal's members must keep open minds until after the evidence has been presented at trial.

If the trial body is appointed by someone interested in the trial's outcome, the courts will find error. Often, the charges

---

[92] NLRB v. Phelps, 136 F.2d 562, 12 L.R.R.M. 793 (5th Cir. 1943); Carroll v. Musicians, Local 802, 235 F. Supp. 161, 52 L.R.R.M. 2950 (S.D.N.Y. 1963); Parks v. IBEW, Local 28, 203 F. Supp. 288, 49 L.R.R.M. 2911 (D. Md. 1962), *rev'd on other grounds*, 314 F.2d 886, 52 L.R.R.M. 2281 (4th Cir. 1963), *cert. denied*, 372 U.S. 976, 52 L.R.R.M. 2943 (1963); Local 3, Bricklayers v. Bowen, 278 F. 271 (S.D. Tex. 1922).

[93] Parks v. IBEW, Local 28, 203 F. Supp. 288, 49 L.R.R.M. 2911 (D. Md. 1962), *rev'd on other grounds*, 314 F.2d 886, 52 L.R.R.M. 2281 (4th Cir.), *cert. denied*, 372 U.S. 976, 52 L.R.R.M. 2943 (1963).

[94] Carroll v. Musicians, Local 802, 235 F. Supp. 161, 52 L.R.R.M. 2950 (S.D.N.Y. 1963).

[95] Semancik v. UMW, District 5, 466 F.2d 144, 80 L.R.R.M. 3475 (3d Cir. 1972); Kiepura v. Local 1091, Steelworkers, 358 F. Supp. 987, 84 L.R.R.M. 2847 (N.D. Ill. 1973); Needham v. Isbister, 84 L.R.R.M. 2105 (D. Mass. 1973); Gulickson v. Forest, 290 F. Supp. 457, 68 L.R.R.M. 2769 (E.D.N.Y. 1968).

[96] Air Line Stewards, Local 550 v. Transport Workers Union, 55 L.R.R.M. 2711 (N.D. Ill. 1963), *rev'd on other grounds*, 334 F.2d 805, 56 L.R.R.M. 2752 (7th Cir. 1964), *cert. denied*, 379 U.S. 972, 58 L.R.R.M. 2192 (1965).

[97] Sordillo v. Sheet Metal Workers, 53 L.R.R.M. 2791 (D. Mass. 1963).

[98] Falcone v. Dantinne, 420 F.2d 1157, 73 L.R.R.M. 2208 (3d Cir. 1969); Stein v. Mutual Clerks Guild of Mass., Inc., 384 F. Supp. 444, 87 L.R.R.M. 2827 (D. Mass. 1974).

are brought by union officials who subsequently appoint the trial body.[99] As Professor Summers has pointed out, the opportunities for abuse in this procedure are obvious:

> Shrewd officers do not sit on trial boards but use their political power within the union to put "yes men" in such strategic spots.[100]

Thus, where an officer who brought the original charges and who testified against the accused member also appointed four out of five members of the trial board, bias was found.[101] Likewise, when the one who appointed the trial body later testified at the trial, bias was found.[102] In contrast, where the governing council preferred the charges and subsequently some of its members served on the trial board, it was held that there was no bias.[103] The distinction apparently lay in the fact that where one person takes action such as preferring charges, he must feel strongly about the issue. When a group makes the same decision by consensus, members of the group are less likely to identify personally with the action.

Although the degree of identification with the action may be less in the latter situation, some identification is probably still there. When possible in such a case, the trial body should be appointed either by officers of the international or by members not involved in preferring the charges. This would diminish the danger of partiality.

It is, of course, improper for the member who prosecuted the case for the union to be present and to participate in the deliberations of the tribunal.[104] This would allow a biased person to participate in the determination of guilt or innocence, and

---

[99] Aaron, *The Labor-Management Reporting and Disclosure Act of 1959,* 73 HARV. L. REV. 851, 874 (1959).

[100] Summers, *Legal Limitations on Union Discipline,* 64 HARV. L. REV. 1049, 1083 (1951).

[101] *See* Lanigan v. IBEW, Local 9, 327 F.2d 627, 628, 55 L.R.R.M. 2315, 2317 (7th Cir.), *cert. denied,* 377 U.S. 979, 56 L.R.R.M. 2480 (1964) stating the district court's holding; the decision was reversed on other grounds.

[102] Air Line Stewards, Local 550 v. Transport Workers Union, 55 L.R.R.M. 2711 (N.D. Ill. 1963), *rev'd on other grounds,* 334 F.2d 805, 56 L.R.R.M. 2752 (7th Cir. 1964), *cert. denied,* 379 U.S. 972, 58 L.R.R.M. 2192 (1965).

[103] Null v. Carpenters Dist. Council, 239 F. Supp. 809, 59 L.R.R.M. 2645 (S.D. Tex. 1965).

[104] Stein v. Mutual Clerks Guild of Mass., Inc., 384 F. Supp. 444, 87 L.R.R.M. 2827 (D. Mass. 1974).

it would allow the prosecutor to participate without giving an equal right to the accused.

It is not necessarily improper for a member of the tribunal to have some involvement with the case before he is appointed to the trial body. For example, a member may serve on the trial body after previously participating in an informal attempt to settle the dispute. The only caveat is that the member must not have prejudged the case.[105]

The courts examine tribunals for a built-in bias against the accused—ideally, none should be present. Realistically, however, a local union with a limited membership and rival factions is unlikely to assemble an impartial trial body. Union constitutions do not usually provide a member with an opportunity for change of venue even if the entire local is prejudiced against him.[106] Since it is probably impossible to prevent some degree of bias in any local union trial, the courts have been forced to borrow the "rule of necessity" from administrative law.

> Under the rule of necessity, disqualified officers are allowed to make decisions when no provision has been made for a substitute tribunal.[107]

---

[105] Falcone v. Dantinne, 420 F.2d 1157, 73 L.R.R.M. 2208 (3d Cir. 1969).

[106] *E.g.,* the *Constitution of the International Brotherhood of Teamsters, Chauffeurs, Warehousemen and Helpers of America,* Art. XIX, § 1(a) (1971) provides:

> Section 1(a). A member or officer of a Local Union charged by any other member of the Local Union with any offense constituting a violation of this Constitution, shall, unless otherwise provided in this Constitution, be tried by the Local Union Executive Board. If the member charged or preferring the charges is a member of such Board, or if a member of the Local Executive Board is unable to attend the hearing for any reason, then the principal executive officer of the Local Union shall appoint a disinterested member as a substitute. If either the President or Secretary-Treasurer of the Local Union is charged or is preferring the charges, or is unable to attend the hearing for any reason, the other officer shall appoint the substitute.
> If both the President and Secretary-Treasurer of the Local Union are charged or are preferring the charges, or for any reason are unable to attend the hearing, the remaining members of the Local Union Executive Board shall appoint the substitutes. Charges by or against a majority of the members of a Local Union Executive Board shall be filed with the Secretary-Treasurer of the Joint Council for trial by the Joint Council Executive Board.

This provision contains no procedure by which an accused member can obtain a change of venue.

[107] K. DAVIS, ADMINISTRATIVE LAW TEXT 253 (3d ed. 1972).

The courts are faced with the task of trying to eliminate all bias while simultaneously allowing the local union to conduct its own affairs. Since these are often mutually exclusive tasks, the courts attempt to tread a middle road. They seek to prevent the most blatant examples of bias, but at the same time, relying on the rule of necessity, they do allow the local union to try its own members.

One solution to the problem of bias adopted by some unions provides for an appeal to an outside review board composed of disinterested parties. Both the United Automobile Workers and the Upholsterers' International Union provide for such public review boards. The members of the boards are prominent citizens of "good repute." They examine a case if, after trial and appeal, the union member is still dissatisfied. This sound approach has not spread to other unions. Those that use it seem to have found it satisfactory, but apparently other unions fear that it would allow too much outside interference with internal union affairs. As a result, it is still the task of the courts to prevent biased tribunals from denying members full and fair hearings.

It is not improper for the accusers to be "persons of influence" within the union. The fact that a union official or a governing council preferred the charges does not mean that the trial will necessarily be biased,[108] since it will normally be the responsibility of someone in power to make the initial accusation.

Evidence

The requirement that the accused be given a full and fair hearing presents several questions relating to evidentiary matters. These include questions of what evidence is admissible, what evidence is excludable, and what evidence will support a guilty verdict.

The first issue is what evidence is admissible at a union trial. The union has broad discretion in this area.[109] However, as one court has said:

---

[108] Falcone v. Dantinne, 420 F.2d 1157, 73 L.R.R.M. 2208 (3d Cir. 1969); Burke v. International Bhd. of Boilermakers, 302 F. Supp. 1345, 72 L.R.R.M. 2749 (N.D. Cal. 1967), *aff'd per curiam*, 417 F.2d 1063, 72 L.R.R.M. 2573 (9th Cir. 1969); Cornelio v. Carpenters, Metropolitan Dist. Council, 243 F. Supp. 126, 59 L.R.R.M. 2722 (E.D. Pa. 1965), *aff'd per curiam*, 358 F.2d 728, 61 L.R.R.M. 2688 (3d Cir. 1966), *cert. denied*, 386 U.S. 975 (1967).

[109] Robinson v. Boilermakers, Local 104, 52 L.R.R.M. 2702 (W.D. Wash. 1963).

Fair play entitles an accused to rely on the written charge made against him . . . [and] limits the trial to proof in support of that charge.[110]

Under this type of standard, the courts have ruled that the evidence not relevant to the charges against the member is inadmissible.[111] In light of Section 101(a)(5)(A)'s requirement of written specific charges, this ruling is correct. If a member has not been accused of violating a rule, it is improper to hear evidence about it. If such evidence were allowed, it would not be clear whether the verdict was based on properly proven charges or on unrelated evidence. Thus, the evidence admitted must be relevant to the violations alleged in the notice sent to the accused.

The second issue is what evidence is excludable at a union trial. As stated earlier, a union has broad discretion in admitting and excluding evidence.[112] The union tribunal may either permit or exclude hearsay testimony.[113] There is, however, a judicial preference in favor of admitting such evidence if it appears relevant.[114] The strict rules of evidence used before courts do not apply before unions. Rather, the evidentiary rules more closely resemble the rules of evidence that apply before an administrative agency.[115] Generally, the members ruling on ad-

---

[110] Allen v. Theatrical Employees, 338 F.2d 309, 315, 57 L.R.R.M. 2368, 2373 (5th Cir. 1964).

[111] Allen v. Theatrical Employees, 338 F.2d 309, 57 L.R.R.M. 2368 (5th Cir. 1964); Eisman v. Baltimore Joint Bd., Clothing Workers, 352 F. Supp. 429, 82 L.R.R.M. 2120 (D. Md. 1972), aff'd per curiam, 496 F.2d 1313, 86 L.R.R.M. 2652 (4th Cir. 1974); Leonard v. MIT Employees' Union, 225 F. Supp. 937, 55 L.R.R.M. 2691 (D. Mass. 1964); Vars v. International Bhd. of Boilermakers, 215 F. Supp. 943, 52 L.R.R.M. 2872 (D. Conn.), aff'd, 320 F.2d 576, 53 L.R.R.M. 2690 (2d Cir. 1963); Nelson v. Painters, Local 386, 47 L.R.R.M. 2441 (D. Minn. 1961).

[112] Robinson v. Boilermakers, Local 104, 52 L.R.R.M. 2702 (W.D. Wash. 1963).

[113] *Compare* Anderson v. Brotherhood of Carpenters, 59 L.R.R.M. 2684 (D. Minn. 1965) (hearsay permitted), *with* Burke v. International Bhd. of Boilermakers, 302 F. Supp. 1345, 72 L.R.R.M. 2749 (N.D. Cal. 1967), aff'd per curiam, 417 F.2d 1063, 72 L.R.R.M. 2573 (9th Cir. 1969) (hearsay excluded).

[114] Anderson v. Brotherhood of Carpenters, 59 L.R.R.M. 2684 (D. Minn. 1965).

[115] The Administrative Procedure Act, 5 U.S.C. § 556(d) (1970) states:
Any oral or documentary evidence may be received, but the agency as a matter of policy shall provide for the exclusion of irrelevant, immaterial, or unduly repetitious evidence . . . .

missibility are not attorneys familiar with the rules of evidence. They are, however, allowed to determine what is relevant and what is not. These members should allow any evidence that appears relevant unless it is so untrustworthy that it has no probative value. On this basis, hearsay evidence would be admissible. As in administrative hearings, a union tribunal may even exclude relevant evidence if it is merely cumulative and the member has already been afforded an opportunity to develop his case fully.[116]

The third issue is how much evidence is necessary to support a guilty verdict. In this area, the Supreme Court, in *Hardeman*, has defined the phrase "full and fair hearing." The Court said that the proper standard of judicial review is that:

> . . . the charging party . . . provide some evidence at the disciplinary hearing to support the charges made.[117]

That "some evidence" is necessary to sustain a guilty verdict is obvious. The Court accepted "some evidence" as the standard for judicial review. It rejected a stricter standard of review (which might, for example, allow a guilty verdict to stand "unless clearly erroneous" evidence was allowed or "substantial evidence on the record taken as a whole" exists to alter the overall record of the case) because it believed that:

> A stricter standard . . . would be inconsistent with the apparent congressional intent to allow unions to govern their own affairs, and would require courts to judge the credibility of witnesses on the basis of what would be at best a cold record.[118]

Both of the Court's reasons for rejecting a stricter standard of review are unsound. Congressional intent, in Title I of the Landrum-Griffin Act, focused on guaranteeing certain rights to union members. Congress did authorize the courts to intervene in the internal affairs of unions when it is necessary to protect these rights. With this in mind, it appears that a stricter standard would be more consistent with the Congressional intent. It is not too harsh to require the union to prove that the member, more likely than not, is guilty of the offense charged.

---

[116] Burke v. International Bhd. of Boilermakers, 302 F. Supp. 1345, 72 L.R.R.M. 2749 (N.D. Cal. 1967) *aff'd per curiam*, 417 F.2d 1063, 72 L.R.R.M. 2573 (9th Cir. 1969).

[117] 401 U.S. at 246, 76 L.R.R.M. at 2546.

[118] *Id.*, 76 L.R.R.M. at 2547.

Such a standard is fairer to the member than the standard of "some evidence."

The Court's concern with lower courts having "to judge the credibility of witnesses on the basis of what would be at best a cold record" is not justified. As was discussed earlier, a transcript, or at least a tape recording that can be transcribed, could be required in all cases. If a transcript exists, then judicial review of a union trial should place no heavier burden on the court than judicial review of other hearings. Since stricter standards of judicial review are regularly used in other areas, there is no reason why they cannot be used in reviewing union trials as well.

A stricter standard of judicial review therefore seems justified. The standard of "some evidence" is too lax. It may result in allowing a union to discipline a member even though the record as a whole shows that he is not guilty.

The Second Circuit, in one case decided after *Hardeman*, interpreted *Hardeman* as *not* saying, ". . . that 'some evidence' to support the charge will preclude . . . judicial review. . . ." [119] Although this conclusion is desirable, it apparently misconstrues *Hardeman*. The Supreme Court said that "some evidence" "is the proper standard of judicial review." [120] It rejected any lesser or stricter standard.[121]

If a member is found guilty of multiple offenses by a general verdict and not all of the charges are supported by some evidence, the entire verdict is void.[122] This follows the principle enunciated by the Supreme Court in *Stromberg v. California*:

> Inasmuch as the case was submitted to the jury as permitting conviction under any or all of the three clauses, and, inasmuch as it is impossible to determine from the general verdict upon which of the clauses the conviction rested, it follows that, if any of the clauses is invalid under the [Federal] Constitution, the conviction *cannot* be upheld.[123]

---

[119] NLRB v. Teamsters, Local 294, 470 F.2d 57, 62, 81 L.R.R.M. 2920, 2924 (2d Cir. 1972).

[120] 401 U.S. at 246, 76 L.R.R.M. 2546.

[121] *Id.*, 76 L.R.R.M. 2547.

[122] Gleason v. Chain Service Restaurant, 422 F.2d 342, 73 L.R.R.M. 2781 (2d Cir. 1970); International Bhd. of Boilermakers v. Braswell, 388 F.2d 193, 67 L.R.R.M. 2250 (5th Cir.), *cert. denied*, 391 U.S. 935, 68 L.R.R.M. 2283 (1968); Pearl v. Tarantola, 361 F. Supp. 288, 83 L.R.R.M. 2901 (S.D.N.Y. 1973).

[123] 283 U.S. at 359 (1931).

In *Hardeman* both Justice White in his concurring opinion and Justice Douglas in his dissenting opinion indicated that they felt that the principle in *Stromberg* applies to union trials.[124] A member disciplined under a general verdict of guilty may well be disciplined for an offense not proved. Even though the evidence may support a guilty verdict on some of the charges, the punishment may have been less severe absent the general verdict and the unproven charges.

Right to Require Union to Follow Its Rules

Most courts which have considered the question have held that the requirement for a full and fair hearing mandates that the union follow its own rules.[125] As one decision stated:

> Having prescribed procedural methods for taking disciplinary action against a member, the District Council was therefore obliged to adhere to such procedures. . . .[126]

This holding is judicious for several reasons. First, if the union has promulgated a rule concerning trial procedure, it presumably believed the rule was fair, reasonable, and desirable. If the union is subsequently allowed to deviate from its rules, the accused may find himself with less protection than the union itself has indicated is fair. For example, suppose the trial board is to consist of eight members and a majority vote is needed to convict a member. This means that the union must convince five members or the accused must convince four. If, in violation of the union rules, the trial is conducted by seven members, then it may be easier for the union to convict the accused. In the latter case, the union must only convince four

---

[124] 401 U.S. at 247, 252, 76 L.R.R.M. at 2547, 2549.

[125] Stein v. Mutual Clerks Guild of Mass., Inc., 384 F. Supp. 444, 87 L.R.R.M. 2827 (D. Mass. 1974); Kiepura v. Local 1091, Steelworkers, 358 F. Supp. 987, 84 L.R.R.M. 2847 (N.D. Ill. 1973); Jacques v. Longshoremen's Local 1418, 246 F. Supp. 857, 60 L.R.R.M. 2320 (E.D. La 1965), *aff'd per curiam*, 404 F.2d 703, 69 L.R.R.M. 2983 (5th Cir. 1968); Leonard v. MIT Employees' Union, 225 F. Supp. 937, 55 L.R.R.M. 2691 (D. Mass. 1964); Rosen v. Painters Dist. Council 9, 198 F. Supp. 46, 48 L.R.R.M. 2721 (S.D. N.Y. 1961), *appeal dismissed*, 326 F.2d 400, 55 L.R.R.M. 2169 (2d Cir. 1964); *contra*, Buresch v. IBEW, Local 24, 343 F. Supp. 183, 77 L.R.R.M. 2932 (D. Md. 1971), *aff'd per curiam*, 460 F.2d 1405, 79 L.R.R.M. 2615 (4th Cir. 1972).

[126] Rosen v. Painters Dist. Council 9, 198 F. Supp. 46, 48 L.R.R.M. 2721 (S.D.N.Y. 1961), *appeal dismissed*, 326 F.2d 400, 55 L.R.R.M. 2169 (2d Cir. 1964).

members that the accused is guilty—one member less than the rules require. The accused, on the other hand, must still convince four members that he is innocent. To allow the union to deviate from its own rule in such a case may divest an accused member of some of the protection which the union itself has found fair.

In addition, when a person joins a union, the courts view him as making a contract.[127] The constitution and bylaws of the union are the terms of the contract. It can therefore be argued that when the union disobeys one of its rules, its disciplinary action is not within the terms of the contract and is therefore not valid.

Limitations on Discipline

One court has held that it is a denial of a full and fair hearing for a union to impose on a member a fine in excess of that allowed by the union's constitution.[128] Imposing a punishment more severe than the union has provided is unfair and hence violates Section 101(a)(5)(C)'s requirement of a full and fair hearing. Due process, too, requires that one's punishment be rationally related to, and in proportion to, one's offense.

Right to Internal Appellate Review

Almost all union constitutions provide for some appeal from the local trial body's decision to some higher body within the union. The adequacy of the union's internal appellate procedures in relation to Section 101(a)(5)(C)'s full and fair hearing requirement has not been the subject of significant litigation. The main area in which the adequacy of the internal appellate procedures has been examined is in the area of requiring a deposit before an appeal may be taken.

The Second Circuit Court of Appeals has approved of the practice of requiring a reasonable deposit before an appeal:

> The Brotherhood may require members seeking to appeal from fines to post a reasonable deposit to prevent overloading the union appeals procedure with frivolous appeals.[129]

[127] NLRB v. Allis-Chalmers Mfg. Co., 388 U.S. 175, 65 L.R.R.M. 2449 (1967).

[128] Stein v. Mutual Clerks Guild of Mass., Inc., 384 F. Supp. 444, 87 L.R.R.M. 2827 (D. Mass. 1974).

[129] Hart v. Carpenters, Local 1292, 497 F.2d 401, 402, 86 L.R.R.M. 2447, 2448 (2d Cir. 1974).

In that case, the deposit was fifty dollars, and there was no claim made that the member was indigent. Thus, the deposit was reasonable in amount and in purpose. Another court, this time a district court, allowed a union to require an appealing member to post a one thousand dollar bond.[130] One thousand dollars is, however, an unreasonably large amount to require a worker to put up as bond. Although such a bond would probably discourage frivolous appeals, it is also likely to discourage valid ones.

JUDICIAL REVIEW

As previously mentioned, the Landrum-Griffin Act provides, in Section 102, for civil enforcement of Title I rights in the federal district courts. There were two areas in which the courts had been confronted with the problem of whether to grant judicial review. First, there was considerable question concerning whether the district courts must yield jurisdiction to the National Labor Relations Board (NLRB) when the union's action was "arguably subject" to the NLRB's jurisdiction. Second, there had been substantial litigation dealing with whether, and to what extent, a member must exhaust his internal union remedies before going to court. Both of these issues eventually came before the Supreme Court for adjudication.

Preemption

In 1959, the Supreme Court, in *San Diego Building Trades Council v. Garmon*,[131] held that when an activity is arguably subject to the NLRB's jurisdiction, "federal courts must defer to the exclusive competence of the National Labor Relations Board."[132] Therefore, if the discipline which a union imposed were arguably an unfair labor practice, the federal courts could not exercise their jurisdiction as granted by Section 102 of the Act, some argued.

In 1971, the Supreme Court, in *Hardeman*,[133] rejected this argument. It found that:

---

130 Carroll v. Musicians Local 802, 235 F. Supp. 161, 52 L.R.R.M. 2950 (S.D.N.Y. 1963).

131 359 U.S. 236, 43 L.R.R.M. 2838 (1959).

132 *Id.* at 245, 43 L.R.R.M. at 2842.

133 401 U.S. 233, 76 L.R.R.M. 2542 (1971).

> The critical issue presented by [the member's] complaint was whether the union disciplinary proceedings had denied him a full and fair hearing within the meaning of § 101(a)(5)(C). . . . [T]his claim was not within the exclusive competence of the National Labor Relations Board.[134]

As the Court pointed out, the factors that justify the preemption doctrine in other instances are lacking in a case like *Hardeman*. The issues raised in such cases are neither "beyond 'the conventional experience of judges'" nor "within the special competence of the NLRB."[135] When Congress passed the Landrum-Griffin Act in 1959, a new body of federal labor law was created. By enacting Section 102, Congress clearly intended the federal courts to handle Title I questions. In addition, the Court explained,

> Since [Section 101(a)(5)] questions are irrelevant to the legality of conduct under the National Labor Relations Act, there is no danger of conflicting interpretation of its provisions.[136]

Hence, the Supreme Court held that the preemption doctrine does not apply to cases dealing with Section 101(a)(5). The reasoning behind this conclusion is persuasive in view of the legislative history of the Landrum-Griffin Act and the needs of the affected employees.

Exhaustion

Section 101(a)(4) of the Landrum-Griffin Act states:

> No labor organization shall limit the right of any member thereof to institute an action in any court, or in a proceeding before any administrative agency . . . *Provided,* That any such member may be required to exhaust reasonable hearing procedures (but not to exceed a four-month lapse of time) within such organization, before instituting legal or administrative proceedings. . . .[137]

When the courts first encountered this section, they had to ascertain whether it was the courts or the unions that had the option of requiring exhaustion of internal union remedies prior to resort to the courts.

---

[134] *Id.* at 237-38, 76 L.R.R.M. at 2543.

[135] *Id.* at 238-39, 76 L.R.R.M. at 2544.

[136] *Id.* at 241, 76 L.R.R.M. at 2545.

[137] 29 U.S.C. § 411(a)(4) (1970).

The issue reached the Supreme Court in 1968 in *NLRB v. Industrial Union of Marine Workers.*[138] The Court concluded that the proviso:

> . . . is not a grant of authority to unions more firmly to police their members, but a statement of policy that public tribunals whose aid is invoked may in their discretion stay their hands for four months, while the aggrieved person seeks relief within the union.[139]

This was based on the Court's belief that free, unimpeded access to the judicial process is necessary. *Marine Workers* was in the context of access to the NLRB, but its rationale applies equally well to access to the courts.

The courts have decided either to require a member to explore his internal appellate remedies for four months or to intervene whenever they believe the case is ripe for adjudication. The decision is within the trial judge's discretion.[140] Since the intent of Section 101(a)(4) is to foster union self-government,[141] there is a preference for exhaustion of prompt and reasonable internal appellate procedures. This allows the union the chance to interpret its rules and then define the issues. It also helps to conserve judicial resources.[142]

There are, however, certain situations in which the courts will intervene prior to the lapse of the four months allowed in the proviso. Thus, the disciplined member will not be required to exhaust his internal union remedies if requiring him to do so would cause him irreparable harm in his job [143] or in the exercise of his Title I rights.[144] Likewise, if resort to the

---

[138] 391 U.S. 418, 68 L.R.R.M. 2257 (1968).

[139] *Id.* at 426, 68 L.R.R.M. at 2260.

[140] Semancik v. UMW, Dist. 5, 466 F.2d 144, 80 L.R.R.M. 3475 (3d Cir. 1972); Giordani v. Upholsterers Union, 403 F.2d 85, 69 L.R.R.M. 2548 (2d Cir. 1968).

[141] Harris v. Longshoremen, Local 1291, 321 F.2d 801, 53 L.R.R.M. 2909 (3d Cir. 1963).

[142] Buzzard v. IAM, Local 1040, 480 F.2d 35, 82 L.R.R.M. 3130 (9th Cir. 1973).

[143] Semancik v. UMW, Dist. 5, 466 F.2d 144, 80 L.R.R.M. 3475 (3d Cir. 1972); Detroy v. American Guild of Variety Artists, 286 F.2d 75, 47 L.R.R.M. 2452 (2d Cir.), *cert. denied,* 366 U.S. 929, 48 L.R.R.M. 2205 (1961).

[144] Semancik v. UMW, Dist. 5, 466 F.2d 144, 80 L.R.R.M. 3475 (3d Cir. 1972); Cefalo v. UMW, Dist. 50, 311 F. Supp. 946, 73 L.R.R.M. 2929 (D. D.C. 1970); Sheridan v. Liquor Salesmen's Union, Local 2, 303 F. Supp. 999, 72 L.R.R.M. 2227 (S.D.N.Y. 1969).

union's internal appeals structure would be futile because it is inadequate or illusory,[145] or because it is controlled by opponents of the disciplined member,[146] the courts will allow the member to seek immediate judicial review. Finally, if the union has consistently taken a position contrary to the accused and has not indicated any change in its position, the member may appeal directly to the federal courts.[147] In these situations, the courts do not see any point in delaying four months before granting the member judicial review.

ATTORNEYS' FEES

Section 102 of the Landrum-Griffin Act provides for civil enforcement of the rights guaranteed to union members by Title I of the Act. It states:

> Any person whose rights secured by the provisions of this subchapter have been infringed by any violation of this subchapter may bring a civil action in a district court of the United States for such relief (including injunctions) as may be appropriate. . . .[148]

In some suits brought pursuant to this section, union members have asked the federal courts to require the unions to pay their attorneys' fees. Originally, the federal courts held that they had no authority to grant such requests.[149] Later, however,

---

[145] Wood v. Dennis, 489 F.2d 849, 84 L.R.R.M. 2662 (7th Cir. 1972), *cert. denied*, 415 U.S. 960, 85 L.R.R.M. 2530 (1974); Buzzard v. IAM, Local 1040, 480 F.2d 35, 82 L.R.R.M. 3130 (9th Cir. 1973); Amalgamated Clothing Workers v. Amalgamated Clothing Workers, 473 F.2d 1303, 82 L.R.R.M. 2313 (3d Cir. 1973); Semancik v. UMW, Dist. 5, 466 F.2d 144, 80 L.R.R.M. 3475 (3d Cir. 1972); Steib v. New Orleans Clerks and Checkers, Local 1497, 436 F.2d 1101, 76 L.R.R.M. 2177 (5th Cir. 1971).

[146] Semancik v. UMW, Dist. 5, 466 F.2d 144, 80 L.R.R.M. 3475 (3d Cir. 1972); Burke v. International Bhd. of Boilermakers, 417 F.2d 1063, 72 L.R.R.M. 2573 (9th Cir. 1969); Fulton Lodge No. 2, IAM v. Nix, 415 F.2d 212, 71 L.R.R.M. 3124 (5th Cir. 1969), *cert. denied*, 406 U.S. 946, 80 L.R.R.M. 2372 (1972).

[147] Amalgamated Clothing Workers v. Amalgamated Clothing Workers, 473 F.2d 1303, 82 L.R.R.M. 2313 (3d Cir. 1973); Semancik v. UMW, Dist. 5, 466 F.2d 144, 80 L.R.R.M. 3475 (3d Cir. 1972); Farowitz v. Associated Musicians of Greater N.Y., Local 802, 330 F.2d 999, 56 L.R.R.M. 2082 (2d Cir. 1964).

[148] 29 U.S.C. § 412 (1970).

[149] *See, e.g.*, McGraw v. United Ass'n of Journeymen of Plumbing, 216 F. Supp. 655, 52 L.R.R.M. 2516 (E.D. Tenn. 1963), *aff'd on other grounds*, 341 F.2d 705, 58 L.R.R.M. 2623 (6th Cir. 1965); Vars v. International Bhd. of Boilermakers, 215 F. Supp. 943, 52 L.R.R.M. 2872 (D. Conn.), *aff'd on other grounds*, 320 F.2d 576, 53 L.R.R.M. 2690 (2d Cir. 1963).

upon further consideration of the issue, other courts began granting such relief when they felt it was "appropriate." [150] The issue was decided by the Supreme Court in 1973 in *Hall v. Cole.*[151]

In *Hall*, the Supreme Court granted certiorari solely to consider,

> . . . whether (1) an award of attorneys' fees is permissible under § 102 of the LMRDA, and (2) if so, whether such an award under the facts of this case constituted an abuse of the District Court's discretion.[152]

After discussing the traditional American rules governing the granting of attorneys' fees, the purpose of the Landrum-Griffin Act, and the Act's legislative history, the Court held, in a six to two decision,

> . . . that the allowance of counsel fees to the successful plaintiff in a suit brought under § 102 of the LMRDA is consistent with both the Act and the historic equitable power of federal courts to grant such relief in the interests of justice.[153]

The Court first pointed out that although the traditional American rule normally does not favor an award of attorneys' fees in the absence of a statutory or contractural authorization, the federal courts, as part of their equitable powers, do have the power to award them when "the interests of justice so require." [154] The Court then indicated two situations in which "the interests of justice" might require that attorneys' fees be awarded.

First, the Court stated:

> . . . that a federal court may award counsel fees to a successful party when his opponent has acted "in bad faith, vexatiously, wantonly, or for oppressive reasons." [155]

---

[150] *E.g.*, Gartner v. Soloner, 384 F.2d 348, 66 L.R.R.M. 2093 (3d Cir. 1967), *cert. denied*, 390 U.S. 1040, 68 L.R.R.M. 2038 (1968).

[151] 412 U.S. 1, 83 L.R.R.M. 2177 (1973).

[152] *Id.* at 4, 83 L.R.R.M. at 2178.

[153] *Id.* at 14, 83 L.R.R.M. at 2182.

[154] *Id.* at 4-5, 83 L.R.R.M. at 2178.

[155] *Id.* at 5, 83 L.R.R.M. at 2178.

The Court emphasized that this is a punitive award based upon the bad faith of the unsuccessful litigant.[156] The Court said that the ". . . 'bad faith' may be found, not only in the actions that led to the lawsuit, but also in the conduct of the litigation." [157]
The second situation in which attorneys' fees may be awarded,

> . . . involves cases in which the plaintiff's successful litigation confers "a substantial benefit on the members of an ascertainable class, and where the court's jurisdiction over the subject matter of the suit makes possible an award that will operate to spread the costs proportionately among them." [158]

The Court found that in *Hall* the plaintiff, by vindicating his own right of free speech, ". . . rendered a substantial service to his union as an institution and to all of its members." [159] The Court pointed out that by vindicating his own right, a successful litigant dispels the "chill" cast upon the rights of others.[160]

Having concluded that the federal courts have the power, as a matter of equity, to grant an award of attorneys' fees, the Court then examined the Act's wording and legislative history to see if it restricted the power of the courts in this area. The Court noted that the Act provides for "such relief (including injunctions) as may be appropriate." It interpreted this phrase to include the awarding of attorneys' fees to a successful plaintiff.[161]

The Court dismissed, as not expressing the view of Congress,

> . . . two isolated comments in the legislative history of Title I—one by Senator Goldwater . . . and the other contained in a dissenting statement to a House Committee Report—expressing the fear that, in the absence of a specific provision for the award of counsel fees, such relief would be unavailable in suits brought under § 102.[162]

The Court found, rather

> . . . that § 102 was intended to afford the courts "a wide latitude to grant relief according to the necessities of the case," and "to

---

[156] *Id.*, 83 L.R.R.M. at 2178-79.

[157] *Id.* at 15, 83 L.R.R.M. at 2182.

[158] *Id.* at 5, 83 L.R.R.M. at 2179.

[159] *Id.* at 8, 83 L.R.R.M. at 2180.

[160] *Id.*, 83 L.R.R.M. at 2180.

[161] *Id.* at 10-11, 83 L.R.R.M. at 2180-81.

[162] *Id.* at 11-12, 83 L.R.R.M. at 2181.

give such relief as [the court] deems equitable under all the circumstances." [163]

Justice White and Justice Rehnquist dissented on the grounds that they,

> . . . would need a far clearer signal from Congress than we have here to permit awarding attorneys' fees in member-union litigation, which so often involves private feuding having no general significance.[164]

The majority's reasoning was sound. Congress apparently meant to grant the federal courts extremely broad powers when it used the phrase "such relief (including injunctions) as may be appropriate." By specifically referring to injunctions, Congress indicated that the courts were allowed to use their equity powers. Such powers, traditionally, have included the right to award attorneys' fees in appropriate situations.

Under the Court's decision in *Hall,* most successful plaintiffs bringing an action under Section 102 of the Landrum-Griffin Act should be able to recover their attorneys' fees. As in *Hall,* by vindicating their Title I rights, the successful litigants are also vindicating the same rights for their fellow union members. Additionally, successful litigants are helping to offset the chilling effects of the union's improper actions. By taxing the union for attorneys' fees, the court will be able, in effect, to spread the cost of the litigation to all of those who benefited from it—all of the union's members. It seems both likely and desirable that such a trend will develop in this area.

CONCLUSION

Section 101 (a) (5) of the Landrum-Griffin Act was enacted to provide due process guidelines that unions must follow in disciplining their members. The section uses general language, and as a result, the federal courts have had the job of defining due process. The safeguards members currently have are fairly comprehensive, but there are several areas in which changes in the Act, or changes in the courts' interpretation of the Act, would be desirable.

First, the courts should recognize that when a union removes an official from his position for his acts as a member, this is discipline

---

[163] *Id.* at 13, 83 L.R.R.M. at 2181.

[164] *Id.* at 16, 83 L.R.R.M. at 2182.

within the meaning of the word as it is used both in Section 101 (a) (5) and Section 609 of the Act. Such an interpretation is consistent with the Act's legislative history and wording. It has the advantage of giving the member more complete protection for his acts as a member. Since there is no need for summary action in such a case, the union is not harmed by a requirement to observe the Act's procedural safeguards.

Second, the Act should be amended to provide that a member may be disciplined only for violating a published, written rule of the union. This would be more just than allowing the union to devise its rules after the fact. If other organizations and governments can write their rules and laws in advance, there is no reason to believe that unions cannot also do so. Such a requirement would not impose any substantial hardship upon the union.

Third, the Supreme Court should reconsider its dictum, concerning transcripts, in *Hardeman*. Although requiring a transcript could impose excessive costs on the union, a tape recording would be inexpensive and would provide the member with more protection from unjust punishment. A transcript or recording would allow the union's internal appellate bodies and the courts to review the union trial more thoroughly and fairly than by using only current testimony. A transcript or recording would be helpful in examining the union trial for procedural defects, bias, or lack of evidence. The courts should decide that a "full and fair hearing" requires a transcript or, at a minimum, a tape recording.

Finally, the Supreme Court should reconsider the quantity of evidence that a court must find, upon review, to uphold a union's guilty verdict against a member. A requirement for an "unless clearly erroneous" or a "substantial evidence on the record taken as a whole" standard would not impose too harsh a standard on the union. At the same time, such standards would give the union member more protection for his valuable membership rights. It is fair to require the union to prove, at least as more likely than not, that the member is guilty of the offense charged. Moreover, such a standard of judicial review would not impose too heavy a burden on the courts. In many other areas, the courts use such standards when reviewing cases.

CHAPTER V

The Current Role of State Courts

Although the passage of federal legislation controlling union discipline of members has reduced the importance of similar state common law, it has not replaced that state common law entirely. Under the Supreme Court's holding in *NLRB v. Allis-Chalmers Manufacturing Co.*,[1] unions have the right to bring suits against their members, in state courts, to enforce fines. Some unions now provide for such court enforcement in their constitutions.[2] As a result, the member may find that the state common law regulating union discipline of members is extremely important to him.

Additionally, even after the Supreme Court's holding in *Amalgamated Association of Street Employees v. Lockridge*,[3] state courts are allowed to hear cases dealing with purely internal disputes between a member and his union. As already noted, the Labor-Management Reporting and Disclosure Act of 1959 (Landrum-Griffin Act)[4] does not limit the state courts' right to hear such cases.[5] Thus, in cases dealing with purely internal disputes,

---

[1] 388 U.S. 175, 65 L.R.R.M. 2449 (1967).

[2] *E.g.*, the *Constitution of the International Brotherhood of Teamsters, Chauffeurs, Warehousemen and Helpers of America*, Art. XXVI, § 1 (1971) provides:

ARTICLE XXVI
SAVING CLAUSES

Section 1. The provisions of this Constitution relating to the payment of dues, assessments, fines or penalties, etc., shall not be construed as incorporating into any union-security contract those requirements for good standing membership which may be in violation of applicable law, nor shall they be construed as requiring any employer to violate any applicable law. However, all such financial obligations imposed by or under this Constitution and Local Union Bylaws (and in conformity therewith) shall be legal obligations of the members upon whom imposed and enforceable in a court of law.

[3] 403 U.S. 274, 77 L.R.R.M. 2501 (1971). *See* Chapter II, note 6, *supra*.

[4] 73 Stat. 519 (1959), *as amended*, 29 U.S.C. §§ 401-531 (1970).

[5] LMRDA § 103, 29 U.S.C. § 413 (1970).

86

a member may find that he is afforded more protection by the state common law than by federal statutes. If so, he may bring suit to state, rather than federal, court.

This chapter examines the current role of state courts in the regulation of union discipline of members. It focuses primarily on the enforcement of union fines and on the areas in which state protection of the members' rights is broader than federal protection.

COURT ENFORCEMENT OF FINES

The Supreme Court, by its decisions in *Allis-Chalmers* and in *Scofield* v. *NLRB*,[6] has held that a civil court may enforce a union-imposed fine against a member if such fine is not for violating a rule that is contrary to public policy. In the last two decades, and particularly since the Court's decision in *Allis-Chalmers,* unions have begun taking members to court to enforce fines.

Enforceability

As the Supreme Court pointed out in *Allis-Chalmers,*[7] the possibility of judicial enforcement of such fines has been recognized at least since *Master Stevedores' Association v. Walsh* was decided in 1867.[8] In that case, however, court enforcement of fines was provided for in a bylaw. Recently, the courts have had to decide whether court enforcement is permitted in the absence of such a constitutional provision or bylaw. The first case to hold that a fine is court enforceable without such a constitutional provision or bylaw was not decided until 1958.[9]

In almost every case that has dealt with the issue, the courts have allowed judicial enforcement of fines regardless of whether such enforcement was provided for in the union's constitution or bylaws.[10] Uniformly, they have based their decisions on the con-

---

6 394 U.S. 423, 70 L.R.R.M. 3105 (1969).

7 388 U.S. at 182 n. 9, 65 L.R.R.M. at 2451 n. 9.

8 2 Daly 1 (N.Y. 1867).

9 Local 756, UAW v. Woychik, 5 Wis. 2d 528, 93 N.W. 2d 336, 43 L.R.R.M. 2741 (1958).

10 *E.g.,* Walsh v. Communications Workers, Local 2336, 259 Md. 608, 271 A.2d 148, 75 L.R.R.M. 2629 (1970); North Jersey Newspaper Guild Local 173 v. Rakos, 110 N.J. Super. 77, 264 A.2d 453, 74 L.R.R.M. 2487 (1970); Jost v. Communications Workers, Local 9408, 13 Cal. App.3d Supp. 7, 91 Cal. Rptr. 722, 76 L.R.R.M. 2475 (1970).

tract theory. They view the relationship between the member and
his union as contractual. The terms of the contract are the constitution and bylaws,[11] and when the member breaches the contract,
the union is said to have a right to sue for damages.

This reliance on contract theory, although appealing, is un-
merited. The contract theory was developed by the courts to
justify their intervention into internal union affairs. Its purpose
was to allow the courts to review union discipline of members to
prevent injustice *to the member.* The "contract" is a legal fiction.
Close examination reveals that under traditional contract law no
contract exists. The "terms" often are vague; [12] they often may
be changed unilaterally.[13] The person joining the union may not
intend to form a contract. Even if he does intend to do so, he
may not be contracting voluntarily; he may believe that full membership is required as a condition of employment.[14]

> In short, membership is a special relationship. It is as far removed
> from the main channel of contract law as the relationships created
> by marriage, the purchase of a stock certificate, or the hiring of a
> servant.[15]

The courts have taken a theory which they formulated apparently
to help the member and have, instead, used it against him. Their
action is difficult to support.

---

[11] *See generally,* Summers, *Legal Limitations on Union Discipline,* 64 HARV.
L. REV., 1049 (1951).

[12] *E.g.,* the *Constitution of the International Ladies' Garment Workers'
Union,* Art. 20, § 1(i) and (l) (1971) provides:

> A member may be censured, fined, suspended, expelled or otherwise
> disciplined . . . (i) for any action or conduct detrimental to the interests
> of the I.L.G.W.U. or a subordinate organization; . . . (l) for any action
> or conduct unbecoming to a member which occurs in connection with his
> membership in the I.L.G.W.U. or employment in its jurisdiction; . . .

the *Constitution and By-Laws, Amalgamated Clothing Workers of America,*
Art. XI, § 1(b) (1974) provides:

> Any member shall be subject to discipline who is found guilty . . . of
> . . . conduct detrimental to the welfare of the Amalgamated.

[13] Summers, *Legal Limitations on Union Discipline,* 64 HARV. L. REV. 1049,
1055 (1951).

[14] *See* Union Starch & Refining Co., 87 N.L.R.B. No. 137, 25 L.R.R.M. 1176
(1949), *enforced,* 186 F.2d 1008, 27 L.R.R.M. 2342 (7th Cir. 1951), *cert.
denied,* 342 U.S. 815, 28 L.R.R.M. 2625 (1951), in which it was held that
an employee may be required by the collective bargaining agreement to pay
the union an initiation fee and periodic dues, but he may not be required
to join the union.

[15] Summers, *supra* note 11, at 1056.

In only one state, Washington, has judicial enforcement of fines been held improper.[16] Even there, it is not clear whether all court enforcement is banned or only enforcement on the facts of a particular case. In one case, the court found that the union constitution provided that a member could be suspended or expelled for nonpayment of a fine. Interpreting the provision narrowly, the court held that suspension or expulsion were exclusive remedies and that, under the contract, court enforcement of fines was precluded. This interpretation has been rejected by other courts.[17] Another court within Washington has indicated belief that court enforcement may be acceptable when the union's constitution or bylaws authorize it.[18]

The Supreme Court of Kansas has also indicated a hostility towards court enforcement.[19] Relying on the contract theory, that court held that where the union constitution did not contain an authorization for the union to expel a member for violating its rules, the union was prohibited from expelling him. Based on this reasoning, this court might also hold that a union may not enforce a fine in court unless judicial enforcement is authorized in the union's "contract."

In light of the contract theory that the state courts use, the courts should not allow court enforcement of fines unless it is provided for in the union's constitution or bylaws. Under traditional contract theory, ambiguous language is construed against the party supplying the form—usually the stronger party. Therefore, if the courts are going to rely on a contract theory, vague or ambiguous language in a union's constitution or bylaws should be construed against the party supplying the form—the union— and in favor of the member. If the contract does provide for certain sanctions, such as suspension, expulsion, or fines, these should be construed as the only enforcement mechanisms. Unless court enforcement of fines is specifically provided for in the "contract,"

---

[16] Retail Clerks Local 629 v. Christiansen, 67 Wash.2d 29, 60 L.R.R.M. 2389 (1965); United Glass Workers' Local 188 v. Seitz, 65 Wash.2d 640, 58 L.R.R.M. 2543 (1965).

[17] Local 248, UAW v. Natzke, 36 Wis.2d 237, 153 N.W.2d 602, 66 L.R.R.M. 2439 (1967). The court indicated that it thought that Washington's law, that a remedy provided in a contract is exclusive, is a minority view.

[18] Teamsters, Local 524 v. Smith, 87 L.R.R.M. 2763 (Wash. Super. Ct. 1974).

[19] Cunningham v. Independent Soap & Chemical Workers, 486 P.2d 1316, 78 L.R.R.M. 2193 (Kan. 1971).

it should not be allowed. Unfortunately, most courts that considered the issue ignored or rejected this argument.

Generally, with or without expressed authority in a constitutional provision or bylaw, unions have been allowed to obtain judicial enforcement of their fines. The only general exception occurs when imposition of the fine is an unfair labor practice; then court enforcement of the fine will be denied.[20]

Size of Fine

The Supreme Court, in *NLRB v. Boeing Co.*,[21] held that the imposition of an unreasonably large fine is not an unfair labor practice.

> Issues as to the reasonableness or unreasonableness of such fines must be decided upon the basis of the law of contracts, voluntary associations, or such other principles of law as may be applied in a forum competent to adjudicate the issue. Under our holding, state courts will be wholly free to apply state law to such issues at the suit of either the union or the member fined.[22]

As indicated above, the state courts have viewed the fines as part of contract law.

In a number of states, members have argued that the fines should not be enforced because they represent penalties or forfeitures for breaching the contract. Such penalties or forfeitures should be viewed as contrary to public policy and not allowed.[23] This argument has met with virtually no success. The courts have generally viewed reasonable fines as the equivalent of liquidated damages; only unreasonable fines have been equated to penalty charges.[24] One court indicated that it viewed the fine as an en-

---

[20] Teamsters, Local 524 v. Smith, 87 L.R.R.M. 2763 (Wash. Super. Ct. 1974).

[21] 412 U.S. 67, 83 L.R.R.M. 2183 (1973).

[22] *Id.* at 74, 83 L.R.R.M. at 2186.

[23] Communications Workers, Local 603 v. Jackson, 84 L.R.R.M. 2689 (Okla. 1973) ; Walsh v. Communications Workers, Local 2336, 259 Md. 608, 271 A.2d 148, 75 L.R.R.M. 2629 (1970).

[24] Communications Workers, Local 603 v. Jackson, 84 L.R.R.M. 2689 (Okla. 1973) ; UAW, Local 283 v. Scofield, 183 N.W.2d 103, 76 L.R.R.M. 2433 (Wis. 1971) ; Walsh v. Communications Workers, Local 2336, 259 Md. 608, 271 A.2d 148, 75 L.R.R.M. 2629 (1970).

forceable debt.[25] Another indicated that it would examine the size of the fine to see if it is "cruel and unusual punishment." [26]

There is a general requirement that the fine be reasonable in size.[27] In almost all of the cases adjudicated, the courts have found the fines reasonable.[28] Of the seven examples of court inquiry into the reasonableness of fines given in *Boeing,*[29] there was only one case, *Farnum v. Kurtz,*[30] in which the size of the fine was found unreasonable. In one case, the Supreme Court asserted that a fine was reduced because it was excessive.[31] The state court, however, did not reduce it because of harshness of penalty but because, as a result of a peculiar rule governing internal appellate review, the fine made exhaustion unreasonable. In a second case in which the Supreme Court asserted that a fine was reduced because it was excessive, the state court again did not reduce it because of harshness of penalty, but because one of three charges was not supported by the evidence.[32]

In determining reasonableness, few guidelines have been offered. Apparently, the burden is on the member to prove the fine is not reasonable.[33] In determining the reasonableness of a fine, one court indicated that it considered the nature of the offenses, the manner in which the member profited from them, and current economic conditions.[34] In holding a fine unreasonable, another court indi-

---

[25] Local 248, UAW v. Natzke, 36 Wis.2d 237, 153 N.W.2d 602, 66 L.R.R.M. 2439 (1967).

[26] Farnum v. Kurtz, 70 L.R.R.M. 2035 (Los Angeles Mun. Ct. 1968).

[27] Walsh v. Communications Workers, Local 2336, 259 Md. 608, 271 A.2d 148, 75 L.R.R.M. 2629 (1970); North Jersey Newspaper Guild Local 173 v. Rakos, 110 N.J. Super. 77, 264 A.2d 453, 74 L.R.R.M. 2487 (1970); Farnum v. Kurtz, 70 L.R.R.M. 2035 (Los Angeles Mun. Ct. 1968).

[28] The financial impact may, to some extent, be reduced because a fine paid by a member to his union is generally tax deductible if the member itemizes his deductions. Rev. Rul. 69-214, 1969-1 CUM. BULL. 52.

[29] 412 U.S. at 76 n. 12, 83 L.R.R.M. at 2186-87 n. 12.

[30] 70 L.R.R.M. 2035 (Los Angeles Mun. Ct. 1968).

[31] McCauley v. Federation of Musicians, 26 L.R.R.M. 2304 (Pa. Ct. of C.P. 1950).

[32] North Jersey Newspaper Guild Local 173 v. Rakos, 110 N.J. Super. 77, 264 A.2d 453, 74 L.R.R.M. 2487 (1970).

[33] Walsh v. Communications Workers, Local 2336, 259 Md. 608, 271 A.2d 148, 75 L.R.R.M. 2629 (1970).

[34] North Jersey Newspaper Guild Local 173 v. Rakos, 110 N.J. Super. 77, 264 A.2d 453, 74 L.R.R.M. 2487 (1970).

cated that it looked at the harm to the union, the amount that the accused would have to earn (before taxes) to pay the fine, and the fact that courts are traditionally lenient to first offenders in misdemeanor cases.[35]

STATE PROTECTION

There are several areas in which the state courts afford an accused member more protection than the federal government under Title I of the Landrum-Griffin Act. When an accused or his attorney is preparing to file a suit against a union, he should consider which available forum offers the maximum protection to the member, bearing in mind that a choice of forum does not require a choice of substantive law.

Protection for Officers

The federal courts have interpreted Section 101(a)(5) of the Landrum-Griffin Act,[36] which provides procedural rules for union discipline, as not protecting an officer from discipline by means of suspension or removal from office.[37] Some of the courts have afforded the officer-member limited protection under Section 609 of the Act.[38] The state courts, however, have often gone farther. They have treated officers as members and found that an officer may not be disciplined by his union unless it has observed the normal procedural safeguards.[39] Since these safeguards are fairly inclusive,[40] this offers union officials substantially more protection than they receive from the federal courts.

Violation of Union Constitution or Bylaw

The Supreme Court, in *Boilermakers v. Hardeman*,[41] ruled that the Landrum-Griffin Act does not prohibit a union from disci-

---

[35] Farnum v. Kurtz, 70 L.R.R.M. 2035 (Los Angeles Mun. Ct. 1968).

[36] 29 U.S.C. 411(a)(5) (1970).

[37] *See* the discussion of this topic in Chapter IV, *supra*.

[38] 29 U.S.C. § 529 (1970).

[39] Hod Carriers Local 89 v. Miller, 62 L.R.R.M. 2835 (Cal. Dist. Ct. App. 1966); Ice Mach. Independent Employees Ass'n v. Swartzbaugh, 78 L.R.R.M. 2473 (Pa. Ct. of C.P. 1971).

[40] *See generally*, Summers, note 11, *supra*.

[41] 401 U.S. 233, 76 L.R.R.M. 2542 (1971).

plining a member for conduct not forbidden by any written rule of the union. Thus, a member has no federal cause of action if the union so disciplines him. Under state law, however, it is well settled that a member may only be disciplined for violating a constitutional provision or bylaw of his union.[42] Thus, he will usually have a state cause of action.

Evidence

The Supreme Court's decision in *Hardeman* indicated that the correct standard for judicial review of discipline cases is "some evidence." Based on Professor Summers's studies, however, state courts go far beyond this by taking additional testimony [43] and reweighing all of the evidence.[44] As such, in a state court, an accused member is more likely to be found not guilty because the union has not adequately proved its case.

Exhaustion

The federal courts have developed fairly consistent rules determining when exhaustion is not required before bringing an action.[45] State courts, however, have developed flexible, inconsistent rules.[46] Thus, a member who does not think that a federal court will assert jurisdiction over his case because he has not exhausted his internal union appeals, may find that the state courts will not require him to exhaust his appeals.

CONCLUSION

Although federal legislation has reduced the importance of state law in union discipline cases, it has not eliminated it. The state law may still be important to a union member for two reasons.

First, a member's union may try to enforce a fine against him in a state court. Relying on the contract theory, the state courts have

---

[42] McGinley v. Milk & Ice Cream Salesmen, 351 Pa. 47, 40 A.2d 16 (1944); Sullivan v. Barrows, 303 Mass. 197, 21 N.E.2d 275, 4 L.R.R.M. 849 (1939).

[43] Summers, *supra* n. 13, at 1085.

[44] Summers, *The Law of Union Discipline: What the Courts Do in Fact*, 70 YALE L. J. 175, 185 (1960).

[45] Semancik v. UMW, Dist. 5, 466 F.2d 144, 80 L.R.R.M. 3475 (3d Cir. 1972). *See* the discussion on exhaustion in Chapter IV, *supra*.

[46] *See* Tesoriero v. Miller, 274 App. Div. 670, 88 N.Y.S. 2d 87, 23 L.R.R.M. 2611 (1949).

generally allowed unions to enforce their fines in court even when the union's constitution and bylaws contain no clause providing for court enforcement. Although this has been permitted by most of the courts which have considered it, allowing such court enforcement does not seem justified. The contract theory, which was developed to protect the union member, has now been reversed and used against the member. Moreover, if the union's constitution or bylaws do provide specified sanctions for certain offenses, then, under traditional contract law, the "contract" which the union provided should be construed narrowly and the specified sanctions should be viewed as exclusive.

When a union does try to enforce a fine in a state court the courts have expressed their willingness to examine the reasonableness of the fine. They have not developed any uniform test, but they look at all of the facts and circumstances. They have indicated that they look at the nature of the offense, the manner in which the member profited from it, the harm to the union, the current economic conditions, the amount the accused would have to earn to pay the fine, and the fact that courts are traditionally lenient to first offenders in misdemeanor cases.

The second reason that state law may be important to a union member is that, in some instances, it may offer him more protection than the federal law. As a result, if a member desires to bring an action, he should ascertain whether the state or federal courts will offer him a better forum.

For example, state law generally provides union officers and employees more protection from summary removal from office than the federal law. Along similar lines, state law normally prohibits discipline except for violations of the union's constitution or bylaws. Federal law has no such restriction. Additionally, state courts tend to be more willing than federal courts to examine the evidence. Moreover, state courts have developed less consistent rules regarding exhaustion than have the federal courts. As a result, a member might be able to convince a state court, rather than a federal court, to hear his case at an early date.

CHAPTER VI

Summary and Recommendations

When a union decides to discipline a member, it must work within the limits that Congress and the judicial system have established. Basically, the union may discipline a member for any conduct that violates a valid union rule.

The validity of the union rule is determined by the interest that it promotes and by public policy. If the rule promotes a legitimate union interest and is not against public policy, it is valid. It may be enforced against all members, including supervisors, to the extent they engage in more than minimal rank and file work. The enforcement mechanisms which a union is allowed to use include resort to the courts for judicial enforcement of fines.

When imposing discipline upon a member, the union must meet minimum due process requirements. Generally, this means the member must be given written specific charges, a reasonable time to prepare his defense, and a full and fair hearing. These terms have been developed rather fully by the courts. Both federal and state laws define due process. If union disciplinary proceedings are to be free of fault, they must observe both laws. These are not conflicting, but they do vary sometimes in their requirements.

Currently, the primary fault of the substantive law is the failure of the courts to recognize that judicial enforcement of fines should be considered an unfair labor practice. Both the legislative history and the statutory provisions of the Taft-Hartley Act dictate that such enforcement be construed as a unfair labor practice. In fact, support for such a position can be found both in Congressional debates and in Section 8(b)(1)(A). Ideally, the Supreme Court will eventually reconsider its contrary holding in *Allis-Chalmers*.

In addition, Congress should enact legislation requiring a union, when recruiting new members, to disclose fully the rights and the duties, the benefits and the obligations, of membership. In order for a union to discipline a person, he must have been a union member at the time he violated the union rule. In some instances, it is not clear whether the employee was a member. In a union shop, an employee is required to pay dues even if he is not a union member. In order to help an employee make the optimal decision, the union should be required to reveal all of his choices and their consequences. This would abet a clear determination of his status as a union or nonunion member. If he chooses not to join, his dues should be equal to his fair share of the bargaining costs in accordance with the rationale for charging him any dues.

A fundamental improvement in handling union discipline could be effected if the National Labor Relations Board would prohibit the inclusion in a collective bargaining agreement of a union security clause which expressly states that an employee must become and remain "a member in good standing." At present, a union and employer can include a legally unenforceable provision which seriously misleads employees as to their rights. In order to enforce the statute, the NLRB should require that union security clauses correctly state what can be legally required of the employee.

A major problem in the federal procedural law is the Supreme Court's holding in *Hardeman* that a member may be charged with violating a rule not specified in the union's constitution and his conviction will not be set aside if there is "some evidence" to support it. The Court should have recognized that due process requires that one not be charged with an offense that is not proscribed. Likewise, a conviction for an offense should not be allowed to stand whenever there is "some evidence" to support it. To determine guilt or innocence, a weighing of all of the evidence is necessary. It is unjust to let a conviction stand when the evidence, taken as a whole, clearly shows the accused is innocent. Yet under the Supreme Court's decision in *Hardeman*, such a conviction may stand. No valid public policy reasons exist for allowing a trial for the violation of a rule not in the union's constitution or bylaws, or for permitting a conviction to stand when the record as a whole shows the person is innocent.

The other problem in the procedural law is that the Supreme Court, in a footnote in *Hardeman*, implied that a transcript is not required at a union trial. If there is to be adequate review by internal appellate bodies or by the courts, a record of the trial proceedings is vital. It is the only way the court can ascertain exactly what happened at the trial. The Supreme Court should, at some future date, consider this issue directly. Recognizing the cost of a transcript might be prohibitive for some unions; perhaps the Court could settle for a compromise such as requiring either a transcript or a tape recording of the trial. If a party believes that a transcript rather than a tape recording is needed, that party could then bear the cost of having the tape transcribed.

The effects of these faults in the federal procedural law, however, can in part be avoided by bringing an action in state court. State courts have consistently required that discipline be imposed only for violation of a constitutional provision or bylaw. In reviewing the evidence of such a violation, they have shown a great willingness to reweigh the evidence and to reconstrue the facts when justice so requires.

Federal legislation has added to the protections afforded to the employee in his relations with unions. Such protections would be enhanced if the recommendations set forth above were followed—recommendations more consistent with Congressional intent than current limiting judicial interpretations.

Index of Cases

Racial Policies of American Industry Series